It's Not Your Grandma's Deliverance

It's Not Your Grandma's Deliverance

Sandy Renner

It's Not Your Grandma's Deliverance
Copyright © 2023 by Sandy Renner. All rights reserved.

No part of this publication may be reproduced, stored in a retrieval system or transmitted in any way by any means, electronic, mechanical, photocopy, recording or otherwise without the prior permission of the author except as provided by USA copyright law.

Scripture quotation marked "NAS" are taken from the New American Standard Bible, Copyright 1960, 1962, 1968, 1971, 1972, 1973, 1975, 1977, 1995 by The Lockman Foundation. Used by permission. All rights reserved.

The opinions expr essed by the author are those of Sandy Renner.

Cover design by Rebeccacovers of FIVERR
Interior design by Aalishaa of FIVERR
Editing by Pamela Scholtes

Published by The Fiery Sword Publications, Lexington, SC, United States of America

ISBN: 978-1-952668-43-2 (softcover)
ISBN: 978-1-952668-44-9 (hardcover)

- Books › Religion & Spirituality › Occult & Paranormal › Supernatural
- Books › Religion & Spirituality › Religious Studies › Counseling
- Books › Religion & Spirituality › Religious Studies › Fundamentalism

Table of Contents

Dedication vii
Endorsements ix
Foreword xiii
Introduction 1

PART ONE: WHY WE DO WHAT WE DO 5

Chapter One: Three Faces of Me 7
Chapter Two: My Life-Changing Experience 13
Chapter Three: Who Needs It? 23
Chapter Four: I Have Jesus, Isn't That Enough? 29
Chapter Five: A Three-Part Being 35
Chapter Six: Spirit versus Flesh 41
Chapter Seven: Let Freedom Rule 49

PART TWO: HOW TO APPLY GOD'S WORD 55

Chapter Eight: Confused Identity 57
Chapter Nine: Demons in People? No Way! 63
Chapter Ten: God's Plan, Man's Choice 69
Chapter Eleven: Living This Life 75

Chapter Twelve: The Unseen Kingdom 81
Chapter Thirteen: Where Do I Begin? 89
Chapter Fourteen: Who Is Qualified? 95
Chapter Fifteen: Getting Prepared 103
Chapter Sixteen: Why Deliverance? 109
Chapter Seventeen: What To Look For 121
Chapter Eighteen: Steps 131
Chapter Nineteen: Ministry Form/Checklist 143

    How to Read the Bible with Purpose 151
    Author Bio 153

Dedication

This work is dedicated to the church on fire! But what does that really mean? As some describe it, the church on fire would be a place where singing is lively, perhaps the gifts of the Spirit flow abundantly. We look at the church in Acts and think it is a place where we speak in tongues, and anyone who does not stand to their feet with hands waving probably is not a church on fire. We see the church as a gathering place of Believers coming together to worship and fellowship. Some churches are defined by the work they do in the community. Others are defined by their doctrine of dress and the order of service on Sunday morning. Some might argue that church must be held on Saturday. Still, others may believe it may not be a real church if they don't have services in a traditional setting. We often judge what type of church a building may represent according to the name or denomination described on the sign on the front lawn. But what does God say the church is and is supposed to produce? Before we investigate the Scriptures, let's settle what the fire is about.

We all know what fire is and what it causes. We think of it as destructive in most cases. Fire in the Scriptures defines it as *"destructive judgment for the disobedient."* Other meanings are described as being a purifier, cleansing agent, and power source. In the Gospel of Luke, John the Baptist says that when Jesus comes, He will baptize in the Holy Spirit and fire. Hebrew describes God as a consuming fire.

DEDICATION

Acts describes tongues of fire resting on the Believers on the Day of Pentecost. 1 Corinthians tells us that all our work will be tested by fire, and the quality of that work will be revealed whether it is worthy of eternal value. Peter tells us that our faith is tested by fire. I believe it is safe to say that a church on fire would indicate the presence of God and the power of the Holy Spirit cleansing and refining the individuals which make up the body of Christ.

The church is not a building or a selected group of people; instead, it is the extension of the power of God present and active on the Earth. Worship is not what we do on a selected day of the week. It is an overflow of a consecrated and dedicated life serving God's agenda to show Him to a lost and dying world, revealing His glory. According to Scripture, the church is an entity of life that has the power to restrain evil on Earth. How are we doing? *It's Not Your Grandma's Deliverance* is only a resource to help us rid ourselves through the power of the Holy Spirit of anything that keeps us from walking in the freedom Christ died to give us. Let's become a unified church on fire so that the world might know Him.

> "That He might present to Himself the church in all her glory, having no spot or wrinkle or any such thing; but that she would be holy and blameless (Ephesians 5: 27)."

Endorsements

As a minister of God's Kingdom, I can confidently say that most, if not all, pastors, counselors, ministry leaders, and ministry teams will encounter people who, no matter what approach they try, can't seem to break free from their bondages of addictions, mental and emotional challenges, poverty, and so much more. In her book *It's Not Your Grandma's Deliverance*, Sandy Renner has done an excellent job approaching the topic of deliverance and inner healing simply and biblically that any pastor, ministry leader, Christian counselor, or layman can understand, learn, and apply to people needing freedom. This book is for such a time as this when dark is getting darker, suicides and other mental health issues are increasing at an alarming and frightening rate, and addictions are affecting almost every household. It's a book I believe would benefit all pastors, ministry leaders, Christian counselors, and church prayer and ministry teams. Jesus paid a high price through suffering and dying to set people free. Deliverance and inner healing go hand-in-hand. They are Kingdom keys that, if considered and applied, would significantly damage the kingdom of darkness by freeing the captive prisoners. I hope and pray that those who read this book will consider purchasing additional books to pass out to their pastors, leaders, counselors, and friends across denominational lines. ~ **Brenda Dukes, Founder & Instructor of Odyssey of the Ark and Kingdom of Heaven Conferences**

ENDORSEMENTS

With the release of this book, Author Renner has released her heart and passion for the wholeness and wellness of the body of Christ. She has an intelligent yet home-spun way of reducing the confusing, religious, and some would say *"frightening"* language of deliverance into a conversational tone accessible to all believers. I am so grateful to have this resource from someone so gifted in this essential ministry. It could not have come at a more crucial moment in the church's life as it is beset with demonic oppression from every quarter. I will recommend this essential book to every pastor and lay minister I know. It is a little book revealing a big Redeemer! To quote Sandy, *"Remember: there are no little demons and more importantly, there is no little Holy Spirit!"* ~ **Pastor Chris Snellgrove, Walnut Grove Methodist Church and Co-Director of Hope Mountain Ministries**

Sandy Renner's book, *It's Not Your Grandma's Deliverance*, is a must-read and beneficial to incorporate into every church's discipline. In this era of gross darkness, it is incumbent for the church to give place for the Light of God to shine brighter and be a beacon of hope for the lost and confused. This book offers simple but imperative information and instructions for every believer to live a life of freedom in Christ, thus pushing back darkness through faith, hope, and love. ~ **Lorrie Lawrence, Transformation Ministries**

It's Not Your Grandma's Deliverance is a timely manual for those desiring to minister more effectively to see the captive set free. The necessity for a scriptural resource to equip and prepare is even more paramount as the Spirit of God is raising up a new end-time generation. Prophetic Teacher and Author Sandy Renner draws on her years of experience to bring an insightful and thoughtful basic instructional deliverance manual. She has accepted the difficult task of presenting a complex subject in a simple and easy-to-understand manner. Any pastor or leader with a biblical understanding will find this a practical guide to initiate deliverance ministry and inner healing.

More importantly, Author Renner has conveyed the necessity of seeking and learning by Holy Spirit's guidance when ministering to those needing freedom. The Spirit of God is raising up a new generation. The need for such scriptural resources to help equip and prepare us for an end-time setting to free the captives is now! ~
Linda Frazier, Co-Laborer in God's Kingdom

Foreword

It's Not Your Grandmother's Deliverance—are you picturing your grandmother chasing you around the kitchen with a wooden spoon? Or perhaps sitting you down to *"straighten you out."* Well, this is definitely not that! What exactly is deliverance? The Oxford Dictionary defines deliverance as *"the action of being rescued or set free."* That is a great starting point.

Galatians 5:1 tells us that it is for freedom that Christ set us free. Stand firm, then, and do not let yourselves be burdened again by a yoke of slavery. I firmly believe Jesus died just for me to be set free and you, too.

Has your mind ever been so cluttered that you cannot thread two thoughts together, let alone retain them? Have you ever been so angry or bitter about someone or a situation that you just can't let it go? How about the anxiety you see reflected not only in yourself but also in your children. If you have answered *"yes"* to any of these questions, you might need *It's Not Your Grandmother's Deliverance*.

Author Renner has been a critical player in the freedom I currently walk in. When I was doing everything I knew to do, she revealed there was so much more. I was so bound up with a lifetime of hurts, confusion, and wrong choices. I had opened the door to the occultic world and didn't know how to make it stop.

FOREWORD

My *"mess"* started as a teenager reading horoscopes and tarot cards. This opened the door to the unseen. As an adult, I thought I was so wise. I never used an Ouija board because I knew they were evil. I did, however, gradually dabble in many other areas that seemed to bring answers to years of confusion, such as palm reading, past life regression, spirit guides, and automatic writing, to name a few.

I had no peace or privacy—EVER! Can you imagine feeling you are never alone? I can't fit a lifetime of wrong choices and hurt in just a few paragraphs, but I kept doing all I knew to do to protect myself. In the process, spiritually, I built high, strong walls around my mind and heart as protection. It wasn't until Sandy and some much-loved brothers and sisters in Christ helped me through the deliverance process that I fully understood I had walled myself in and everything else out.

As you walk this path of discovery, you will discover how to apply God's Word to your current situation in an applicable way right where you are. In recognizing and speaking God's truth into your circumstances, you will walk in more freedom than you can imagine. God is so perfect, and He is waiting to guide you through His Word on this journey of self-discovery and, more importantly, this journey of God's discovery.

Gods Blessings on your journey! ~ **Carole Doran**

Introduction

I have been asked many times to write a deliverance manual, but I only recently became interested. My friend, ministry partner, and publisher, Alexys V. Wolf, pushed me to write this book. She even came up with the name, *"It's Not Your Grandma's Deliverance."* She knows I come from a Pentecostal background and have moved into deliverance ministry for many years. Still, I was not convinced I needed to write a book. However, when God tells you it's time, you do it.

You may be asking, *"Who does this concern?"* My answer is, *"You!"* If you are not a born-again believer, this book will help you understand why you are not living a fulfilling life. Perhaps you are living what you consider a good life but struggle within and can't find answers. This book will give insight into an action plan. Of course, you must recognize your need for change. Your real need is a Savior, Jesus Christ. I pray you will see He is the answer for your life.

I wrote this book mainly for pastors and church leaders or anyone with influence in other people's lives. Perhaps you are a Bible study leader, Sunday School teacher, small group leader, or one many come to discuss their life difficulties over coffee. Whatever your position, you have a responsibility and ability to lead others to the freedom Christ came to give us.

Every pastor has encountered someone who exhibits behavior that seems untouched through preaching and teaching God's Word.

INTRODUCTION

You sit across from them in your office and sense something out of order, and all the counseling in the world is not penetrating. The truth is, you cannot cast out a broken heart or heal a demon [demonic influence on someone].

I have been in ministry for over forty years and have been involved in deliverance ministry for most of that time. I have learned many things through the course of this strange ministry. I stopped doing it for a long time because I became frustrated at seeing strongholds broken off people, and they seem to end up in worse shape from a lack of true discipleship.

Deliverance is not a cure-all; one must learn how to walk in freedom. I take issue with a lack of seasoned and mature believers willing to help mentor others. The first problem is a sincere lack of mature believers, and the second is the unwillingness to invest their time to help others. There may be several reasons for this. Perhaps, believers are not maturing because they have soul wounds themselves that have never been addressed. The unwillingness to invest is often from selfishness, which explains the immaturity. Lack of understanding or teaching on how to lead others to freedom may keep those able and willing from working in this ministry. I want to address these issues by providing information and training so this ministry will be user-friendly, regardless of denomination.

This book is not to confront or accuse ministers of not doing their best. Sadly, preaching the Word and personal counseling is not enough to bring believers into spiritual maturity. However, people are broken for many reasons and unable to move beyond their pain to receive all Christ died to give. Rather than balk at something new or refuse ministry a bit different than you are used to, let's learn and do all we can to make it available to the body of Christ. Deliverance and inner healing ministry are other avenues to finding total freedom and becoming the glorious Church.

Suppose after reading this book, you would like further training or understanding. In that case, I will make myself available to help answer questions. One of my suggestions would be to take a group of mature and willing believers within your Church through training in administering this freedom. Afterward, there needs to be a system in place to mentor and/or disciple individuals to walk in their newfound freedom.

I sense an intense need to implement a system to help believers become spiritually healthy and stable. It is sad to say, but I have witnessed many cases of Christians not acting much differently than those who do not confess Christ as Savior. They may attend Church and occasionally read their Bible, but when faced with conflict, their response is based on how they feel, what they think, and what they want rather than Christ's model. It is time to get our act together. Why? It does not take a biblical genius to see the world's increasing darkness. Social chaos, political corruption, sexual confusion, violence, rampant drug usage, and emotional and mental disorders are rising. Significant denominations are splintering, churches are allowing the world's perversions to entertain congregations, Christians are unsure of what they believe as truth, science is running amuck, and so on. Yes, some of these things have always been, but the increasing rate is alarming.

We, the Church, are supposed to be a light in a dark world. We should be the salt of the Earth and lead the way to righteousness. Empowered by Holy Spirit, we are supposed to be the restrainer of evil. Yet, more times than not, we are following the culture. We are to embrace all people; we are not to embrace their lifestyles. We don't understand proper boundaries. I pray and hope for a better day, but are we prepared for what may be coming? If darkness continues to increase, as the Bible indicates, and deception will rule the day as the Bible clearly defines, are we ready to stand? The Apostle Paul, in Ephesians, instructs that warfare is to stand.

The Church at large is so deficient in spiritual truth that I am concerned with society's growing deception that we will be unable or unwilling to see the truth. The Lord strongly impressed me that

INTRODUCTION

from the soulish defilement most Christians operate in, it will get in the way of seeing through deception. It is time to get our souls healed and freed from anything un-Christ-like so that we will not fall for the great deception headed our way.

I urge all pastors, leaders, and mature believers to allow Holy Spirit to search our hearts and ensure we can stand in the evil day. Like Christ, we must be sure our soul's enemy has nothing to hold in us. We must be willing to help our fellow servants in this fight against evil to be prepared with clean hands and a pure heart. Most spiritual leaders get so busy that we often don't see how the dysfunctions of life cling to us and defile our thinking.

In *"It's Not Your Grandma's Deliverance,"* I seek to remove the hype, fear, weirdness, and sensationalism of deliverance ministry. I hope to simplify the process to help ourselves and others come to the freedom Christ died to give. Even if you have previously doubted this type of ministry or thought it was too weird to consider, I pray you will read and see how this might help you bring yourself and others to soul wellness.

> Now may the God of peace Himself sanctify you entirely; and may your spirit and soul and body be kept complete without blame at the coming of our Lord Jesus Christ (1 Thessalonians 5:23).

PART ONE

Why We Do What We Do

CHAPTER ONE

Three Faces of Me

In 1957, a film was released starring Joanne Woodward. *"The Three Faces of Eve"* portrays a woman claiming multiple personalities. She was sometimes an ordinary, plain, timid housewife. Occasionally she would become a wild seductress acting entirely unlike the woman everyone saw daily. She sometimes exhibited a radical transformation into a sophisticated, educated, gracious lady. The movie's point demonstrates how the three lifestyles brought confusion and pain into Eve's life. The movie's plot followed a psychiatrist as he worked with her to integrate these personalities into one whole person.

Today, this is called dissociative identity disorder or DID for short. I don't know how likely it is for this phenomenon to occur, nor am I qualified to diagnose a person that may suffer from this. I suppose anything is possible. I have ministered to many people who can hide much of who they are deep down. We all have things we don't want anyone to see. We have what I call *"everybody's face," "We need to impress"* face, and of course, *"Don't push my buttons because you won't like it"* face.

"Everybody's face" is the one we show those with whom we are comfortable. Mostly, it is who we are in our everyday normal life. The *"need to impress"* face is one we exhibit when we feel the need to be more sociable or when we need to show better behavior than

normal. We put on this face around those we don't see often, or the circumstances warrant our company manners. This face usually appears when the preacher visits, at funerals, church, work, or when we find ourselves with others possessing a higher living standard, more money, or higher education. Finally, there is the *"don't push my button"* face. This attitude arises when we feel we are being judged. Insecurity is the culprit for exhibiting aggression. We don't like the feeling of being inferior or insecure. When the pressure is on, we react, and it doesn't work for our good. No matter how many faces we have, it is time to remove the masks and allow Holy Spirit to heal us and bring us to wholeness.

As a child and teenager, I was often the class clown—not because I was funny, but to hide my insecurities. Most people who know me would laugh at that admission. Outwardly, I tried to be the tough girl. I didn't cry easily. I was mouthy and defensive. Being the clown was the alternative to being the tough girl. When it didn't work, I became violent. I would hurt you physically before you could hurt me. It took me years to realize these reactions came from shame and insecurity. Being poor and having alcoholic parents left me feeling that my life was abnormal. This taught me to hide my identity. I found out later in life very few have what we consider to be *"normal"* lives. We all have something we want to hide.

Once I came to Christ, from good teachers, I grew in understanding. Still, it did little to resolve my emotional issues. I discovered most Christians have a lot of emotional baggage. I was determined to learn how someone could know the Scriptures and mature in faith yet still be emotionally insecure. Most of us don't realize how broken we are.

Walking this faith journey means we must pick up our cross daily and die to ourselves. This is why I am so passionate about getting others to experience freedom from the wreckage of our souls. I was desperate to understand how to have the life described in the Scriptures. I wanted to know how to live powerfully rather than pitifully. My journey in deliverance ministry began early in my faith journey. As I spiritually matured, I realized deliverance comes in many forms. Most of what we call *"deliverance"* is inner healing. Deliverance sometimes involves dealing with evil spirits; however, this is not to be scary or mysterious, nor is it reserved for a few weird people to perform in some back room. Jesus spent a good bit of time casting out demons. As Christians, we should all be involved in helping our brothers and sisters in Christ obtain freedom.

Maybe you have wondered why you behave in ways you know are wrong as a Christian. You vow to do better; you have every good intention, but the moment your button is pushed, an emotional explosion erupts. You are left wondering, *"What is wrong with me?"* You may be unwilling to accept responsibility and blame the other person for pushing you into an argument. Whatever the reason, we must understand how we are made to get to the root of our behavior. This is what we will discover in the following chapters.

Notes

CHAPTER TWO

My Life-Changing Experience

Forty-plus years ago, I had an experience that changed my life. I became born-again. I suppose every person who receives Christ as their Savior expects transformation to be like the Apostle Paul's; his conversion is told in Acts. Many expect they might receive a significant phone call from Heaven or, at the very least, an Earth-shaking experience. However, that is not what happens to the majority who receive this precious gift. Most people regret how they have lived as a deep tug within their hearts draws them to repentance. No matter how one receives the call to Christ, the experience is just as powerful and valid as the life-altering event Saul encountered on the road to Damascus. Saul, who later became the Apostle Paul, was knocked off his donkey and heard the voice of Jesus. It takes something radical to reach some of us. Let me assure you, those who had a more than average experience is not because we are special. It has more to do with our stubbornness and need to be in control. The Lord knows what it will take for each of us.

I wasn't riding a donkey, and I didn't hear the voice of Jesus, but I guess it would be safe to say my salvation experience wasn't within the normal spectrum. Unlike so many, I can't give you the actual date I got saved, although I was around twenty-four years old. I had been raised in a Nazarene denomination. I often attended a Church of God with my grandmother as a young child. Grandma's church was known for shouting excitedly as *"the Spirit fell."* At least, that is what they called it. I was never sure from where He had fallen.

Nevertheless, when He fell, He must have made quite a commotion, as it caused most of the older women, including my grandma, to behave weirdly. They would begin to shake and jiggle, causing their hair to jar loose from their tight buns, and hairpins flying as they would speak in tongues. It didn't seem a big deal; it was just how they did church.

I was used to the Spirit moving through people as they spoke with other tongues, so it wasn't a big issue for me. Years later, Aunt Barbara and my sister, Barbara (Southerners tend to repeat names), came home from a church service. They referred to this service as a crusade, as they talked about the movement of Holy Ghost. They would speak of a man who headed these crusades known as Prophet James Shinn. I didn't have the foggiest notion of what being a prophet meant. I didn't care until they began describing what was happening in these meetings. They talked about how Prophet Shinn would pray, touch someone's forehead, and they would fall as though asleep. This man seemed to hear from God and receive personal information concerning people. They called it prophesying. I had never heard of such things. Speaking in tongues and jumping around as the Spirit fell was one thing. However, in my mind, this new movement the two Barbaras were involved in had to be a cult of some kind.

It is only fair to explain why this was important to me. Every family has a fixer. You know what I mean, someone who feels as if they are the one to straighten out every other family member. That was me. I was the family fixer. Of course, I wouldn't let such a person called a *"prophet"* deceive my family. It was my duty to find out about this person and expose him. I heard he would be back the next week, and I would be there to straighten him out.

Upon finding the place and time of the next meeting, I went inside and sat in the back. That was the only seat available as at least a couple hundred people filled the room. I spotted my aunt and sister in the front row; they were singing and waving their hands in the air. That was okay. I had seen that in my grandma's church. I supposed knowing my grandma did some of those things made it normal. One could sense the energy building as the music got louder. People were shouting and getting excited. Then the show began. The prophet started praying for people, and as expected, they fell to the floor as someone placed large cloths on them to keep them properly covered. He would give some a message from the Lord. I stayed still, waiting, as I rolled my eyes and sighed in sincere disgust.

The prophet waved at the lady playing the organ to take it down a notch or two. I discovered later she was his wife. Then he spoke to the audience calling a name— my name. He said, *"There is someone here named Sandy. God wants you to come up front."* For a moment, I was stunned. I wasn't expecting that, but I didn't move. My mind was racing. I reasoned that with the number of people present and Sandy being a common name, he surely did not mean me. I was wrong. He stepped into the aisle, pointed at me, and said, *"Little black-haired girl, isn't your name Sandy? Come here."* I wasn't about to get emotional; I could figure this out. I wasn't impressed because I thought, *"It makes sense, my aunt or sister saw me and passed him a note."* Yep, I was quite pleased with my assessment. I had it all figured out, so I thought this would be my opportunity to expose him. I got up, walked to the front with exaggerated boldness, and stood before him. With my arms folded in front of me to show him I was not open to any of his shenanigans, I set my face with a look of pure defiance. I thought, *"Okay, big boy, knock me down."* I don't know what I expected him to do in response to my stance, but I didn't expect what he did next. He stood and stared at me for a moment, which seemed like an hour. Turning, he walked to the far corner behind the podium. He put his face in the corner. I was nervous and wondered, *"What is this fruitcake doing?"* He held up his hand, waving it toward me, and ever so softly, said, *"In the name of Jesus."* I kid you not. When those words came out of his mouth, something picked me up at least a couple of inches off the floor as I was hurled backward by this unseen force. I landed on my back, unharmed but shaken to my core! I still wasn't impressed—shaken, but not impressed. I figured it out. He must have hypnotized me, and if I could get my legs to work, I would stare him down. He called for two men to help me and bring me to where he stood. My legs felt like wet noodles, but I couldn't let him see how shaken I was. Then he began to tell me about my childhood in a soft, almost fatherly voice. He said he could see me at seven or eight years old.

He described in detail the bed he saw me sitting on. It was a twin bunk bed with a wagon wheel on the headboard. He even detailed my worn-out bedspread and the green plaid dress I was wearing. He was extremely accurate. I remembered the dress because I only had a few, and it was the dress I wore to get my school pictures taken that year. That was enough to shut down my need to figure it out, but what he said next changed my life. He went on to tell me of a prayer I had prayed in my heart at that age. It was a prayer no one knew of because I never voiced it out loud. I remembered it as if it happened the day before. My childhood was difficult due to my parents, who struggled with alcohol. That prayer was a little girl's plea for God to rescue her. Prophet Shinn went on with the prophecy to tell me about the call on my life and what that call would entail. This time he slightly touched my forehead, and I hit the floor like a ton of bricks! When I got up, I knew I had been born-again. I didn't understand it, but I knew it was true.

James Shinn became my spiritual father and mentor. He taught me things most church people would have difficulty accepting. James taught me about spiritual deliverance. We did what we knew during the early days of learning deliverance. Like most of the Pentecostal movement that I saw growing up in church with my grandmother, there seemed to be a fair amount of emotionalism. Deliverance was similar. There was a lot of screaming at the devil, demanding he come out of the person who supposedly had a devil. Yelling in tongues and laying the big King James Bible on heads was the order of the day. James had a better handle on deliverance than most I watched through the years. Before I get too critical and judgmental, I want to assure you we were at least trying to help Satan's victims. Most denominations would never attempt deliverance for fear of being too weird. This book will help remove the weirdness and get it out of the back room and even out of Hollywood's portrayal. As the title implies, this is not your grandma's deliverance. It's a new day, and inner healing and deliverance is a much-needed ministry that should be incorporated into every church.

Allowing what I learned from James to be a foundation, I continued to seek God on how to change and grow in deliverance ministry. Prophet James Shinn has gone to be with the Lord, but he left me a legacy. I have a responsibility to pass it on. I desire this to guide how to walk our faith journey with victory and freedom from those things keeping us in bondage. Sometimes it includes dealing with demons that work within and influence our life from the outside. More than anything else, deliverance is about receiving inner healing from the brokenness of our souls. You can cast out a demon, but not a broken heart. Knowing the difference and how to effectively deal with both is essential. Demons should never be our focus. Rather, we need a revelation of the goodness of our Father in Heaven and His Son, Jesus Christ. I will be forever grateful to my mentor for teaching me how to know God and His heart to set His people free.

There are two main parts to this book. The first part is to discover why we do the things we do and help us see ourselves more clearly. Our emotional dysfunction keeps us from living the life Christ died to give us. My heart is to teach others how to walk this faith journey effectively. I want to create a fresh opportunity with clear instructions on how to be free from the brokenness of our souls.

The second part will be a deliverance manual with instructions on how to personally apply God's Word and the ministry of Holy Spirit. This is to rid us of emotional bondage and help others walk through the process. The word *"deliverance"* in connection with ministry seems to be negative. Needing deliverance does not make one less spiritual. Seeking deliverance and inner healing indicates that one is willing to do what is necessary to live in freedom to walk in faith, hope, and love. Receiving and walking in deliverance will enable us to be powerful vessels of which Holy Spirit can show the strength of Christ the Savior!

Perhaps you didn't have a grandma who went to church. Even if you did, she might not have attended a church that believed in deliverance. This may be a new subject for you. The title of this book came from a need to show how we all need deliverance from something. These habits can keep us from living in true faith, hope, and love. A woman once declared to my mentor, *"I don't have demons!"* He replied, *"If that is true, then why do you act the way you do?"* If we say we are born-again, yet we continue in a lifestyle or indulge in habits not aligned with biblical standards, we must conclude that we are being rebellious, meaning we continue living by our old standards, not adhering to the new life we have in Christ. This could lead us to believe we only prayed to get us through an emotional difficulty and did not receive Christ by faith. Perhaps we did mean it when we prayed for salvation, but something keeps us from maturing in the faith.

> "Therefore, if anyone is in Christ, he is a new creature; the old things have passed away; behold, new things have come (2 Corinthians 5:17)."

Refrain from confusing this with the process of spiritual growth. You will not immediately become a mature Christian. However, if you repented of your sin from regret of your life choices and, by faith, received the gift of salvation, you will experience a desire to please God. You may not be able to overcome all your bad habits overnight, but there will be a continuous growth of change in the way you behave, think, and speak. If you are not experiencing change through reading God's Word and learning to effectively pray as you sit under solid biblical teaching, you may have spiritual influences from demonic sources. This should not scare you, but it may help explain why you are not receiving God's promises.

In this book, I will help you determine what keeps you from walking your faith journey in freedom. I will also instruct how to get free, stay free, and help others to do the same. Another reason for the title is to help those who have operated in deliverance ministry. If you are still using the same patterns in deliverance as you did decades ago, you may need a fresh approach. Deliverance, like any other ministry, should experience growth and change. It should not be something for a small group to take ownership. Deliverance and inner healing guides should be incorporated into every church ministry. My hope is to initiate a guide to inner healing and deliverance ministry without fear and intimidation. I want to remove the weirdness, at least as much as possible. It is understood that any time we deal with the supernatural, it may get uncomfortable.

> The Spirit of the Lord GOD is upon me, because the LORD anointed me to bring good news to the humble; He has sent me to bind up the brokenhearted, to proclaim release to captives and freedom to prisoners; to proclaim the favorable year of the LORD and the day of vengeance of our God; to comfort all who mourn, to grant those who mourn in Zion, giving them a garland instead of ashes, the oil of gladness instead of mourning, the cloak of praise instead of a disheartened spirit (Isaiah 61: 1-3).

Notes

CHAPTER THREE

Who Needs It?

"Who may ascend onto the hill of the LORD? And who may stand in His holy place? One who has clean hands and a pure heart, who has not lifted up his soul to deceit and has not sworn deceitfully (Psalm 24:3-4)."

You may think, *"I gave my life to Christ. What else is there?"* It is true that when we accept Christ and His gift of salvation, it is a complete release from sin's penalty [eternity in hell]. Our spirit man becomes awakened and alive because Holy Spirit now resides there after accepting Christ. It is as pure as it can be and sealed according to Ephesians 1:13. Is it enough? It is as far as eternity is concerned. However, salvation alone does not eliminate sin's effects within our minds, which involves our will, emotions, memories, and imaginations. A life of sin combined with the results of Adam rebelling against God leaves a residue on how we respond to life's difficulties and relationships. We may escape hell, but too many Christians live substandard to God's desires. Why? We are going to discover the reasons and the solutions.

In Romans 12:2, we are told not to be conformed to this world but to be transformed by renewing our minds. This mind transformation is our responsibility. Thanks be to God; He gives us

Holy Spirit to empower us in this endeavor. We would never be able to do it on our own. Salvation comes only through God's grace. We can't earn it or ever be good enough to acquire it. It is a gift received by faith alone. Nor can we overcome the past without Holy Spirit's help. Our soul reveals the residue of our fallen nature.

How do we begin this transformation? We must first admit we need change. Secondly, we must want change badly enough to pursue it. Deliverance is a never-ending process because life keeps happening. That does not sound fun, but it isn't difficult. The key to finding success is learning how to lay down what we want, think, and feel. When we discover how good life can be under Holy Spirit's leadership, our life's joy will become evident. Old things will be exchanged for wonderful and exciting new adventures.

Many will say they want a better life, stress free from our choices, but we put off doing what we must to acquire the abundant life Christ died to give us. We won't get there by continuing to put off change. Perhaps we don't know how to change, and/or we have something always pulling at us to keep us locked in a destructive behavioral pattern. I will give insight into what those things consist. Once exposed, the solutions will be outlined in a simple delivery format. It is up to every individual to accept responsibility and act upon it. No one can do it for you. Deliverance is not done to you; it is a ministry performed alongside you.

It is simple to answer the question, *"Who needs deliverance?"* We all need it. Deliverance has gotten a bad reputation in the church arena. When some hear the term *"deliverance ministry,"* they get wound in knots and immediately get offended or defensive. This is because many don't believe demons exist. Others know they exist but believe they have insignificant effects on people. Most have difficulty wrapping their minds around demons inside someone, especially a Christian. This is a thought to consider; angels are spirits, demons are spirits, and Holy Spirit is a spirit. My point is, as a Christian, Holy Spirit lives inside us, so why do we find it hard to believe demons also can enter us? The Scriptures bear this. I have not seen angels entering a person in the Scriptures, only demons. Why? My understanding is our soul's enemy, Satan, is like an illegal invader. Satan and his demons defy God's nature. Only God has the right to be inside a believer. Angels in right standing with their Creator, God, would not violate His standards. Demons will if allowed.

We will see this possibility as we progress. We need to understand that deliverance and salvation are the same. They both involve a rescue. Salvation is a rescue from sin's penalty [spiritual death and eventually hell for all eternity]. Deliverance is a rescue from anything that keeps us from receiving all the benefits or promises of Christ. Jesus declared in John 10:10 (NLT) that His purpose is to give us a rich and satisfying life. How many Christians are living this? I suspect very few. This rescue is needed because of our past failures or traumas we experienced throughout our life. We may have had violations against our bodies or emotions by others as well as our personal choices. Christ has given us the right and responsibility to claim all God's promises. This will not be obtained just by quoting Scriptures. We can have the freedom to love and live without reservation, but we must submit everything we are to Him and trust His power to bring change into our lives.

> But we have this treasure in earthen containers, so that the extraordinary greatness of the power will be of God and not from ourselves; we are afflicted in every way, but not crushed; perplexed, but not despairing; persecuted, but not abandoned; struck down but not destroyed (2 Corinthians 4: 7-9).

> Grace and peace be multiplied to you in the knowledge of God and of Jesus our Lord, for His divine power has granted to us everything pertaining to life and godliness, through the true knowledge of Him who called us by His own glory and

excellence. Through these He has granted to us His precious and magnificent promises, so that by them you may become partakers of the divine nature, having escaped the corruption that is in the world on account of lust. Now for this very reason also, applying all diligence in your faith supply moral excellence, and in your moral excellence, knowledge, and in your knowledge, self-control, and in your self-control, perseverance, and in your perseverance, godliness, and in your godliness, brotherly kindness, and in your brotherly kindness, love. For if these qualities are yours and are increasing, they do not make you useless nor unproductive in the true knowledge of our Lord Jesus Christ (2 Peter 1:3-8).

Notes

CHAPTER FOUR

I Have Jesus, Isn't That Enough?

Have you or someone you know ever investigated Christian counseling? Most likely, only Christians, or at least those with some Christian values, will seek it. There are plenty of counselors who specialize in various emotional needs. I pulled a list of Christian counselors just in my immediate area. I was flabbergasted at the considerable number of them. This list did not include pastors who do counseling for their congregations. It leads one to wonder if these folks have a relationship with Christ or, at the very least, ascribe to some biblical applications for their life. Why is it not enough?

Something is amiss for such a large group of available counselors. These professionals would only be in a vocation if it could financially support them. This alone alerts us that many are seeking out help. Counseling often helps us cope with or manage the pain of our past and helps us understand how to get past our hurt.

An example would be anger, counseling may help redirect anger through self-control, but it most likely won't eliminate the problem. Anger and other out-of-control emotions are embedded in the soul. It must be dealt with on a spiritual level. A broken or defiled soul results from sin and can only be healed through Holy Spirit's power.

I want to be concise. It is not wrong to seek professional help. This is not about finding fault or judgment toward those who seemingly cannot get it together. Thank God, He has given gifts of wisdom and helps men and women help others find peace of mind.

> "Where there is no guidance the people fall, but in an abundance of counselors there is victory (Proverbs 11:14)."

Is Jesus enough? This question must be defined before a proper answer can be determined. Jesus certainly is enough to cleanse us from sin and deliver us from sin's penalty [total separation from God]. He is the one and only perfect sacrifice for our redemption.

> "The sting of death is sin, and the power of sin is the Law; but thanks be to God, who gives us the victory through our Lord Jesus Christ (1 Corinthians 15: 56-57)."

Perhaps you have put your trust in Christ but struggle with intense feelings you know are unhealthy or un-Christlike. Stress, anger, jealousy, lust, defensiveness, and unforgiveness are among the many emotions we deal with. We will often mask our behavior by using excuses, such as:

1. It is just the way I am.
2. I can't help how I feel.
3. I try to make those thoughts go away.
4. If they wouldn't make me so mad!
5. I just worry and I can't help it.
6. I'm just a nervous person.
7. People just drive me crazy.
8. My boss is always on me.
9. I didn't do anything wrong, but…
10. My anger just gets the best of me.

These excuses will not hold up if we seriously want to live for Christ. We must come to Christ just as we are, because if we wait until we change or become good enough in our eyes, it will never take place. If we could do it, we wouldn't need Christ. It is a process allowing Holy Spirit to reveal our need for change. Through repentance and cooperation with Him, change will come.

I talk to many people who have known Christ for years, yet they still lack spiritual maturity. When this is brought to their attention, I hear, *"I'm working on that,"* or *"I'm trying. God knows my heart."* You may wonder, *"What is wrong with those things? At least they are aware of their need to change."* The problem is they are only excuses. They probably have been saying the same things for years. How long is long enough to work on an issue? God knows our hearts and sees we deceive ourselves when we think we can do anything to improve ourselves. We believe that if we are *"working on it,"* we don't have to change. We continue that lifestyle because we think we are entitled to those feelings.

> "My old self has been crucified with Christ. It is no longer I who live, but Christ lives in me. So, I live in this Earthly body by trusting in the Son of God, who loved me and gave himself for me (Galatians 2:20, NLT)."

> "Don't you realize that your body is the temple of Holy Spirit, who lives in you and was given to you by God? You do not belong to yourself, for God bought you with a great price. So, you must honor God with your body (1 Corinthians 6:19-20, NLT)."

> AND YOU SHALL LOVE THE LORD YOUR GOD WITH ALL YOUR HEART, AND WITH ALL YOUR SOUL, AND WITH ALL YOUR MIND, AND WITH ALL YOUR STRENGHT (Mark 12:30).

There are so many Scriptures I could quote, but I don't want to overwhelm you. The above verses, alone, show us our responsibility to relinquish what we want, think, and feel. If you are beginning to feel defeated or guilty, hold on. That is not the purpose of this book. I am going to share with you the solutions. However, we must all see our needs clearly. We must go to the root of our dysfunction and get delivered from our worst enemy, often ourselves.

Notes

CHAPTER FIVE

A Three-Part Being

> Now may the God of peace make you holy in every way and may your whole spirit and soul and body be kept blameless until our Lord Jesus Christ comes again (1 Thessalonians 5:23 NLT).

If you read my previous book, *"Cross This Line...I Dare You,"* you will find I went into a lot of detail concerning the soul. I will shorten it, but it might be beneficial for you to read that book. According to the Scriptures, we are a spirit possessing a soul living in a physical body. To be clear, one part of us cannot sin, and the other two remain indifferent. Sin affects us in every way.

Before we receive Christ as our Savior, our spirit is dormant [asleep]. This is from the fall of man when Adam and Eve ate from the Tree of Knowledge of Good and Evil. Afterward, man's spirit was no longer aware of God. When we are born-again, our spirit is awakened because God is a spirit, and He comes to dwell within us. We possess a soul comprised of our will, intellect or mind, emotions or feelings, imaginations, and memories. The soul in the Scriptures is often interchangeable with the heart or mind. It is an information center and a guiding entity for our actions. It is unseen by the physical eye because it is a part of our spiritual being, unlike the brain, which is physical and can be seen and touched. We don't know where the soul's actual location is within our body. Hebrews 4:12 says God's Word acting as double edge sword can separate the spirit from soul. This leads us to believe they are in proximity. Both the spirit and the soul are unseen by the human eye. The physical organ known as our brain will one day die but not our soul or spirit.

We live in a physical body of organs, blood, bones, and all that keeps us alive. Sometimes our body is referred to as *"flesh."* Like our mind and brain—one is spiritual and one is physical. The Scriptures refer to our body as flesh when describing the things our soul tells us what it desires. Our physical body wants and needs material things such as food and water to survive and receives information from our physical brain. Our flesh wants stuff we think we need to be happy. I call this the *"I want, I think, I feel"* syndrome. These are controlled by our souls. Even after we are born-again, the soul will be our ruling force until we allow it to be healed from the sins' effects. The key is to train our soul to behave and desire the things of our born-again spirit.

According to Scripture, all three parts are essential and play significant roles in our physical and eternal spiritual lives. This is why we must learn how to get all three parts living in harmony with God's Spirit. Our problem mainly comes from our broken souls. I often use the analogy of our soul being a trash compactor. When we are small children, we learn how to store emotions with which we don't know how to deal. We push them down and continue this process throughout life. Living in a healthy home environment may teach us how to better deal with emotions, but for those of us who did or do not, dysfunctional emotions become our norm. Emotions are expressed in extremes. Maturing and acquiring education may help us better handle expressing our emotions. However, be aware that the unhealthy and volatile emotions building for years have not disappeared. They are lurking deep within the trash compactor of our souls. The correct pressure or circumstances will cause their presence to be made known.

> "Beloved, I pray that in all respects you may prosper and be in good health, just as your soul prospers (3 John 1:2)."

To better understand how our soul functions, I will take a moment to describe each part:

1. **Mind**: This includes our intellect. This is where information is processed concerning how we relate to people or situations. It is our emotional guide to our unseen senses. It is often referred to as our "*heart*"—not physical—in the Bible.
2. **Will:** This is where we make our decisions about what we will or won't submit. When this is violated through force of any kind, it impacts every part of our being.
3. **Emotions/feelings**: These determine how we relate to ourselves, other people, and God. Whenever our soul is emotionally unhealthy, it will show up in how we respond to others and situations. Unhealthy emotions rule our negative choices.
4. **Imagination**: Because our Creator [God] is a creator, and He made us in His image, He gave us an imagination. An imagination is a story built around an image or picture. God gave us an imagination to create; it is intended to be for our good and His purpose. When our imagination becomes defiled from corrupt information which is fed through our soul and/or our five senses—seeing, hearing, smelling, touching, or tasting—it creates dysfunction in our behavior.
5. **Memories**: These are collective pieces and pictures of information of our past. Every particle of information we obtain through our lives, via our physical senses and soul, real and imagined, help form us. These memories fuel our

emotions. Thus, our choices are often decided by what we have stored in our memories.

God created us with these functions to live a whole and joy-filled life. Through the fall of man, sin entered the world. Adam's separation from God through fear, rebellion, and pride infected every person after him. We are flooded with more information than any other generation. Most of our exposure has not served us well in creating a wholesome environment. Mankind has not improved considering all this information, but it has caused regression as a healthy society. Knowledge is good, but when it is void of wisdom and God-driven guidelines, it brings corruption.

Our soul has been corrupted through our mind being cluttered with copious defiled information. Worldly influence violates our will, causing us to believe we must have certain things to be happy. Our emotions are broken through abusive and unhealthy relationships. Our imagination is tainted with misleading pictures of unrealistic expectations. Memories are distorted through all other defilements of our soul, leaving us to judge people and life events from contaminated information. Out of this confusion, we choose how to live our lives. No wonder divorce, sexual dysphoria, child abuse, mental illness, false religion, political corruption, corporate greed, drug abuse, overused prescribed anxiety medication, and various other evils are continually rising. Is it any wonder we, as individuals, including Christians, live dysfunctional? Is there hope? We still have hope because Christ is still alive and drawing us unto Himself.

> "For God so loved the world, that He gave His only Son, so that everyone who believes in Him will not perish but have eternal life. For God did not send the Son into the world to judge the world, but so that the world might be saved through Him (John 3: 16-17).

Notes

CHAPTER SIX

Spirit versus Flesh

Remember that we are a spirit with a soul that lives in a body. Because we are physical, spiritual, and emotional beings, we are subject to malfunctioning on many levels. We understand this physical body is subject to injury or disease, causing organs to become damaged, resulting in poor health or death. However, when it comes to our compromised emotions, we push them away, compartmentalize them, deny their importance, or take a pill. Our spirit lies dormmate until Christ's gift of salvation has been accepted. This awakens our spirit and is then filled with Holy Spirit and sealed. In other words, it is as healthy and holy as it will ever be.

So, where is the disconnect? You may be thinking, *"I am a Christian. Isn't that enough?"* An authentic relationship with Christ will produce change. The evidence of His character and holiness will become evident through the spiritual maturing process. One might say, *"I've changed. I don't drink, smoke, do drugs, beat my spouse, chase women or men, and I don't cuss much anymore. I go to church and read my Bible, so what is the problem?"*

Relationship with Christ is not measured by what we do or don't do. Doing good works is an overflow of Christ working in and through us. Not doing bad things should also be an overflow of the work of Christ. Relationship with Jesus should cause us to have

His character produced through Holy Spirit. In Galatians 5:20, the fruit exhibited by Holy Spirit is love, joy, peace, patience, kindness, goodness, faithfulness, gentleness, and self-control. Fruit is evidence of how one lives. This fruit should be evident in every born-again believer. Granted, these characteristics of Holy Spirit will continue growing, but if He lives in us, they will be present.

Of course, as these mature, the works of the flesh should become less visible. Works of the flesh, according to Galatians 5:19-21 are sexual immorality, impurity, indecent behavior, idolatry, witchcraft, hostilities, strife, jealousy, outbursts of anger, selfish ambition, dissensions, factions, envy, drunkenness, and carousing. These fleshly characteristics are inherited from Adam, forfeiting his God-given station through his rebellion against God's law.

We do not need a demon to operate in the works of the flesh. We do this from our sinful nature. However, if one who has received Christ cannot fully submit and overcome these practices, they will attract demons. Works of the flesh are sin; demons find a legal way to connect when sin is allowed to reign. This is how it plays out. The physical body is enticed through its five senses—seeing, hearing, touching, smelling, and tasting. When these senses rule our behaviors, it starts working on a spiritual level. This means it begins a process of invading areas of our soul, which is our unseen command center for our flesh. This creates conflict within our emotions [feelings], mind [intellect], will, imaginations, and memories.

Let's use a simple analogy to trail this behavioral pattern. Sally has a sweet tooth; she struggles with a desire to eat sugary foods. It could be from a physical imbalance. However, she does not visit the doctor. Instead, she continues in her struggle. She is overweight from her poor food choices. She fights the urge to overeat and her love of sugary treats. She may hold it down to a single donut if she is with others, but a dozen becomes her norm when alone. As she eats, she tells herself she will start doing better tomorrow. What may be a physical issue becomes an emotional stronghold.

After eating an entire dozen, Sally's soul has been compromised as she feels guilt from her lack of control. Shame overwhelms her as she looks at her overweight body. She feels like an outcast and cannot physically participate in some activities because of her weight. She imagines people are avoiding her, and now feels rejected. One thing leads to another, and she no longer has the will to fight. Her memories are filled with guilt, shame, rejection, fear, and loneliness. Sally's soul became defiled from allowing her senses to entice her to respond to what she wanted and felt and her thoughts of momentary pleasure. Does this mean she has a demon? Not necessarily. However, all those painful feelings will lead her to mental and emotional dysfunction if left unattended. Other out-of-control emotions will develop. Anger, resentment, and self-hatred will emerge. Left untreated, this soul defilement will become a drawing card for demonic activity. Like germs drawn to wounded flesh, demons are spiritual germs drawn to soulish dysfunction.

This is a simple analogy but can be played out in various circumstances. When people are in emotional and mental confusion, they stay there or seek counseling. This can be helpful; however, spiritual issues need to be managed on a spiritual level. Christian leaders need to learn how to address this.

How can Christians do all the right things, endeavoring to be sincere in their faith, yet these works of the flesh continue to cause them to stumble? They read their Bible, pray, and fellowship with other like-minded believers, and they still can't seem to get free. There could be several reasons to explain this shortcoming. Influences can have a negative impact. For instance, if someone has a problem with drugs or alcohol consumption and associates with others who indulge or attend certain places or events where this is promoted, a change must occur where and with whom time is spent. Finding new friends with a lifestyle more in line with the life they are trying to live will prove beneficial.

When we have done all, and know what to do, yet are still plagued with desires that won't subside, we may need intervention. Being a three-part being doesn't negate being one whole person. What we do in our body will impact our soul. Being addicted or using addictive substances places our souls in conflict, which messes with our physical-chemical makeup. Works of the flesh enacted through our physical body will reveal the impurities of a defiled soul. It becomes a cycle challenging to get out of. It may require a ministry of inner healing and/or deliverance. Your mind may be filled with questions if you are new to this ministry. What is deliverance? Is it possible for a demon to be in a Christian? Why would I need inner healing if I am saved? What is the difference between the two? These are all good questions, so let me give an analogy to explain deliverance.

Suppose you work a construction job early in the day and cut your arm. It doesn't need stitches, but it is more than a scratch. You should go to the first aid station, but you're "*the man*," so you wipe the blood and stop the bleeding. You think it's not too bad and continue to work all day. You unrolled your sleeve to keep dirt out so your boss doesn't see it. You don't want to miss work. After a while, you forget about the cut until you get home. You take a shower and feel the sting of soap on the cut. It looks red and irritated, but you wash it and go to bed. The following day, it seems infected, so you put ointment on it and go to work. When you get home, the cut is causing a little pain, and you realize it may need medical attention. But, you are tough and talk yourself into believing it will get better with home care. Before you know it, you are dealing with a deep infection.

Not properly attending that cut allowed an infection to form. That freshly damaged skin and flowing blood began to draw flies and insects that carry germs, screaming, *"Fresh food, come and get it!"* This is a natural explanation of what takes place in the spiritual realm. Whenever a work of the flesh is practiced, and the root of the problem is not adequately addressed, it becomes an invitation to demonic influence. Demons are drawn by dysfunction and works of the flesh. Much like insects carrying germs are drawn to wounded flesh, demons are like spiritual germs drawn to soulish dysfunction. This does not mean every time a person sins, a demon enters. It means that a lifestyle outside of God's Word will open doors for demonic activity. It is an open invitation.

Let's look at it from a soulish and spiritual perspective. Lydia grew up in an unhealthy environment. Her parents fought often, and her mother secretly drank alcohol to cope. She didn't get falling down drunk, but she stayed just tipsy enough that it was not as secret as she thought. She often got tickets for traffic violations and would stumble and fall in public places. This caused Lydia to feel ashamed and insecure. She eventually grew up and married a man who mistreated her. She felt as if she didn't deserve better. She came to know Christ, but she also had a secret drinking problem; not as bad as her mom, or so she thought. She grew spiritually and wanted to give up drinking, but it had a hold on her. She confided in her pastor, and he tried to help and even sent her to a counselor. She felt better being able to tell her secret. The drinking slowed, but she could not completely stop. Why? Why wasn't knowing Christ and getting counseling enough?

During Lydia's formative years, shame and insecurities took a firm root in her soul, damaging her emotions. This led to other problems—shame, insecurities, worthlessness, and deep-seated anger. Alcohol abuse became an escape but created more shame, and more lies developed. These damaged emotions were like that cut on the man's arm. Left untreated, every insect laden with germs and harmful bacteria is drawn to light on that damaged flesh, leaving behind potential infection. When damaged emotions are left without proper attention, it promotes a broken and defiled soul affecting all the other parts. Lydia's will became unable to submit to healing, her intellect was overruled by the memories of shame from her childhood, and her imagination became tainted, leaving her unable to clearly understand her identity in Christ. All she could see was her dysfunction.

Pride was born to hide her shame. Lydia's broken soul called to every other spiritual germ like that untreated cut on the man's arm. Demons are always looking for a person to attach themselves to or enter—they inhabit the soul. A person in a relationship with Christ has a sealed spirit, and demons cannot get in. They are content to occupy one's soul where they have some level of control and/or influence over the person's mind, emotions, will, imaginations, and memories.

Whenever a person has trauma, a broken heart, and/or damaged emotions, it creates soul wounds. This leaves them with the potential for a demon to wreak havoc over them through outside influence or inhabitation. Inner healing is needed for a healthy soul to exist. Once a soul receives healing, if there are demons present, they no longer have a legal way to occupy. This still requires deliverance, as the demons want to stay in their space. The presence of a demon in or attached to a believer does not mean they are evil or possessed. It doesn't have to be complicated, and we get our steps to freedom from God's Word.

I liken the recognition of demon's presence to a fire. When a person has a defiled soul, it is like a slow-burning fire. It may stay hidden and in control, depending on the person. However, when circumstances threaten one's emotional state, it is like someone throwing gasoline on the fire. An outward explosion will occur. Have you ever had someone get on your nerves, and you lose it? It wasn't that bad, but your button got pushed, and you reacted and wondered later why you got so angry. You know you should have been able to deal with it without becoming volatile. Does that mean you have a demon inside you? It is possible, but it might mean you only need inner healing. Let's take the first thing first.

Notes

CHAPTER SEVEN

Let Freedom Rule

All athletes are disciplined in their training. They do it to win a prize that will fade away, but we do it for an eternal prize. So, I run with purpose in every step. I am not just shadowboxing. I discipline my body like an athlete, training it to do what it should. Otherwise, I fear that after preaching to others I myself might be disqualified (1 Corinthians 9:25-27, NLT).

Apostle Paul used the example of running a physical race to show the importance of being prepared to win and finish life's race. My husband, Ray, is a cyclist. He trains daily, getting up at 4 every morning, and either rides his bicycle outdoors or his indoor stationary bike, depending on the weather. He also does strength training. He eats food his body needs at the appropriate times. He knows what his body requires to function at its maximum. Everything in his day is filled with the understanding it may affect his performance in an upcoming race. He is racing against brutal competition, and although he wants to win and trains accordingly, his real goal is to stay in the race and finish as well as he can. An enormous amount of time and attention goes into this sport. The proper clothes, shoes, and accessories must be worn to get the best results.

In the Scriptures above, Apostle Paul says, *"I run with purpose in every step. I am not just shadowboxing."* He was not speaking of a physical race but his spiritual journey. A committed athlete doesn't waste time, energy, and resources on things that work against their ability to win. As Christ's followers, we should take our spiritual race even more seriously. After all, we are running for an eternal prize.

It is time for the household of faith members to start behaving like kings and priests of God instead of broken, busted, and disgusted vagabonds. According to Scripture, we are ambassadors for Christ. We are supposed to rule this planet as we one day will rule God's Kingdom under His guidance. This is our practice ground. It is time to get over ourselves and our past to lead others to Christ but with successful Kingdom minds. To do this, we must get our souls healthy and whole. Don't get caught up in fear or unbelief of demons invading your mortal being. Who cares about what we must rid ourselves to win the prize of Christ?

> Not that I have already obtained it or have already become perfect, but I press on so that I may lay hold of that for which also I was laid hold of by Christ Jesus. Brethren, I do not regard myself as having laid hold of it yet; but one thing I do: forgetting what lies behind and reaching forward to what lies ahead, I press on toward the goal for the prize of the upward call of God in Christ Jesus (Philippians 3:12-14).

Beloved, it is time for us, as the body of Christ, to stop living in yesterday's pain, hurts, and deception. I don't teach that you should forget the wrongs done to or by you or shove them in some unseen trash compactor. We must face them and rid ourselves of unnecessary baggage. If we get serious, stop worrying that we might be found out, and take these steps by faith, we will find freedom and discover how to enjoy our spiritual journey. Let's eliminate the trash that has kept us from being all we can be.

Being apprehensive or even a bit scared of this type of ministry is easy. Still, all we must lose is insecurity, fear, anger, unforgiveness, rebellion, pride, the need to show how right we are, and out-of-control competitiveness. These are only a few things that keep us from God's promises. So, what if we must disengage a demon that we don't want to admit we have. Just think of them as spiritual leeches. We wouldn't leave a physical leach on our body to drain our life. Let's not allow our religious or fearful beliefs to keep us in bondage.

I will show you in Scripture where Jesus and Apostle Paul cast out demons. It is incredible how many of us lived in bars or places where fights broke out, many took chances of being involved in sexual activities where we could get sexual diseases, and/or many activities that could have caused us grave harm, and we say we fear this type of ministry! Come on, we didn't mind trying everything the world had to offer and look where that got us! Let's dare to take Jesus at His Word. Let's get healed in our souls and see how our physical bodies might respond in a newfound health. We will walk through inner healing. If a demon is interfering, we will take care of that as well because we have the authority of Christ.

Notes

PART TWO

How To Apply God's Word

CHAPTER EIGHT

Confused Identity

Sin is our foundational enemy, but we know as Christ-followers, Jesus went to the cross to atone for mankind. His perfect blood was shed so that we might be saved, rescued, and delivered from sin's penalty. Sin means *"a transgression of God's law and a vitiated [faulty or defective] state of human nature in which the self is estranged from God."*

Salvation is God's gift through the atonement of Jesus Christ. Sin is anything outside God's law or violating His holiness. Many today want to know how far the envelope of sin can be pushed without violating God's standard. We would never ask that question, but our behavior indicates our motivation. This is a sign of residue left on our souls from our sinful lifestyles. While our sin has been totally forgiven, its residue keeps us in a battle between good and evil. We may be heaven-ready from Christ's salvation, but are we able to live on Earth evident we are one with the Lord? Trying to live as a Christ-follower but continually polluting our souls causes us to lose or, at the least, confuse our God-given identity.

> And God did not spare the ancient world-except for Noah and the seven others in his family. Noah warned the world of God's righteous judgment. So, God protected Noah when he destroyed the world of ungodly people with a vast flood.

> Later, God condemned the cities of Sodom and Gomorrah and turned them into heaps of ashes. He made them an example of what would happen to ungodly people. But God also rescued Lot out of Sodom because he was a righteous man who was sick of the shameful immorality of the wicked people around him. Yes, Lot was a righteous man who was tormented in his soul by the wickedness he saw and heard day after day. So, you see, the Lord knows how to rescue godly people from their trials, even while keeping the wicked under punishment until the day of final judgment. He is especially hard on those who follow their own twisted sexual desire, and who despise authority. These people are proud, and arrogant, daring even to scoff at supernatural beings without so much as trembling (2 Peter 2:5-10 NLT).

I chose to share this Scripture portion to show how sin or unrighteous acts can inflict torment on the soul. The Scripture indicate Lot was righteous, but to what he was exposed defiled his soul. He had to be delivered. This occurred in the Old Testament before Jesus. God had to physically deliver Lot because God did not inhabit people. Today under the New Testament covenant, we are filled with Holy Spirit if we are born-again. What we lend to our ears and eyes will impact our souls. Satan and his demons torment us from within through our minds or souls. Deliverance must come from within through our cooperation with Holy Spirit. God's Word makes apparent rebellion against God will not be tolerated. There will come a day of accountability. The last portion of this Scripture indicates what I believe to be the root of all evil influence, pride, fear, and rebellion against God's authority.

> "When the woman saw that the tree was good for food, and that it was a delight to the eyes, and that the tree was desirable

> to make one wise, she took from its fruit and ate; and she gave also to her husband with her, and he ate (Genesis 3:6)."

> "For all that is in the world, the lust of the flesh and the lust of the eyes and the boastful pride of life, is not from the Father, but is from the world (1 John 2:16)."

We see from these two Scriptures that our flesh desires to rule. Our flesh gets its information through the soul. This information enters through our five senses. This is the *"I want, I feel, I think"* desire that must be transformed to meet God's standards. Back to the Genesis account of Adam and Eve's rebellion against God's instruction, we see Adam's response to God asking him where he was.

> "Then the Lord God called to the man, and said to him, "Where are you?" He said, "I heard the sound of You in the garden, and I was afraid because I was naked; so, I hid myself (Genesis 3:9-10)."

If you have read my two previous books, *"One Law"* and *"Cross This Line… I Dare You,"* you will remember I expounded on the Genesis account in detail. It tells of the foundation laid by the evil one for the destruction of mankind. Three leading spiritually damaging spirits were loosed over mankind that we struggle with today. Fear, rebellion, and pride were given authority by Adam to rule. Every dysfunction of our soul is rooted in these three categories. We will see if this theory is correct. Adam said, *"I was afraid because I was naked; so, I hid myself."*

Pride gives birth to lust—the tree was a delight to Eve's eyes. Her desire to be wise outside God's provision was rooted in pride. She felt as if she deserved it. Rebellion was given birth through lust.

Fear paved the way for shame. Adam felt something he had never experienced before eating the tree's fruit. He had been naked all along in front of a Holy God, and it never occurred to him to feel shame until pride and rebellion exposed his nakedness. God's glory had been Adam's covering. Now shame became its replacement. Pride enabled man to believe he deserved something that God forbade. Rebellion was his response to God's instruction, which produced his need to hide. This was Adam's way of declaring his independence from God. Pride declares, *"I'll take care of myself. I don't need You!"*

Now we have a list of soul violations—pride, rebellion, fear, shame, lust, and refusal to take responsibility. Adam blamed his wife and God for his sin. How many people do you hear justifying their wrongs by blaming someone else? The Scripture from 2 Peter 2 shows how sin has escalated. Lot was dealing with sexual perversions, mocking, arrogance, violations of spiritual authorities, and rebellion, and we are dealing with this and more today.

Notes

CHAPTER NINE

Demons in People? No Way!

You may think, *"Is it true demons can be inside us?"* Let's go to the Scriptures to see. A mute, demon-possessed man was brought to Him as they went out. After the demon was cast out, the mute man spoke, and the crowds were amazed, saying, "*Nothing like this has ever been seen in Israel* (Matthew 9:32-33)." In this instance, the man was unable to speak. Once Jesus cast out the evil spirit, the man could talk. This clearly shows how a physical disability was directly from an evil spirit.

> But after hearing of Him, a woman whose little daughter had an unclean spirit immediately came and fell at His feet. Now the woman was a Gentile, of the Syrophoenician race. And she kept asking Him to cast the demon out of her daughter. And going back to her home, she found the child lying on the bed, the demon having left her (Mark 7: 25-26; 30).

This account is disturbing because an evil spirit was in a child. How does that happen? We are given limited details; however, we will discuss later how spirits can enter a person regardless of age. In the synagogue, there was a man possessed by an unclean demon, and he cried out with a loud voice, "*Let us alone! What business do we have with each other, Jesus of Nazareth? Have You come to destroy us? I know who You are- the Holy One of God* (Luke 4:33-34)!"

Wait a minute! A person in church was inhabited by a demon. There was more than one inhabiting this man. The spirits recognized Jesus and understood He had the power to deal with them. *"It happened as we were going to the place of prayer. A slave woman with a spirit of divination met us, bringing great profit to her masters by fortune-telling. She followed Paul and us and cried out repeatedly, saying, 'These men are bondservants of the Most High God, who are proclaiming to you a way of salvation.' Now she continued doing this for many days. But Paul was greatly annoyed and turned and said to the spirit, "I command you in the name of Jesus Christ to come out of her!" And it came out at that very moment* (Acts 16: 16-18).

This passage shows someone other than Jesus dealing with a possessed woman. She was heavily involved in witchcraft. Was she praising them or mocking them? She acknowledged their position in God and the message they proclaimed. Either way, Paul did not need a demon to verify or exalt them, as their validation came from God's Spirit. He shut the demon up!

> So, they arrived at the other side of the lake, in the region of the Gerasene's. When Jesus climbed out of the boat, a man possessed by an evil spirit came out from a cemetery to meet him. This man lived among the burial caves and could no longer be restrained, even with a chain. Whenever he was put into chains and shackles-as he often was-he snapped the chains from his wrists and smashed the shackles. No one was strong enough to subdue him. Day and night, he wandered among the burial caves and hills, howling and cutting himself with sharp stones. When Jesus was still some distance away, the man saw him, ran to meet him, and bowed low before him. He shrieked, "Why are you interfering with me, Jesus, Son of the Most High God? In the name of God, I beg you, don't torture me!" For Jesus had already said to the

spirit, "Come out of the man, you evil spirit." Then Jesus demanded, "What is your name?" And he replied, "My name is Legion, because there are many of us inside this man." Then the evil spirits begged him again and again not to send them to some distant place. There happened to be a large herd of pigs feeding on the hillside nearby. "Send us into those pigs," the spirits begged. "Let us enter them." So, Jesus gave them permission. The evil spirits came out of the man and entered the pigs, and the entire herd of about 2,000 pigs plunged down the steep hillside into the lake and drowned in the water (Mark 5:1-13, NLT).

This is one of the most interesting passages about demon possession. We will look at the particulars of this demonstration of demons. This man had extreme physical strength, and he was obviously mentally disturbed. The man ran out to meet Jesus. It could have been just the man's desperate need to get help from Jesus. We don't know if the man knew Jesus outside the demon's knowledge, but the demons clearly recognized Him. They called Him by name. The demons were many, at least 2000 inhabited the man. The name the demon gave Jesus was "*Legion*," a military term indicating thousands.

I know that seems impossible and extreme. I have never encountered someone with that many demons during my deliverance ministry. However, I have seen as many as several hundred. These demons not only recognized Jesus, but they undoubtedly knew Him as the Son of God. They also admitted He had power over them. Jesus granted them entrance into the pigs. Why would He do that? Spirits don't die but look for a breathing body to inhabit. Jews were forbidden through the Law to eat pork. These pigs were what we would consider black market pigs. The pigs were driven mad when the evil spirits entered them, or they would rather be dead than live with evil inside them. No matter, Jesus knew that would get rid of the pigs, even if it was through suicide. If you read the rest of this account, you will find the man known in the community was found sitting in his right mind after Jesus set him free.

> "Then Satan entered Judas, called Iscariot, one of the Twelve (Luke 22:3)."

This is a whole new level of possession. It was not a demon but the head of evil himself, Satan. This was not an ordinary citizen or sinner but one of the chosen disciples. In reading the entire story, you will find Judas, who betrayed Jesus, tried to return the money he received for turning Jesus over to the authorities. He was sorry, but he did not repent.

Notes

CHAPTER TEN

God's Plan, Man's Choice

I have a strong belief that if we want to understand God and His thinking, we must go back to the beginning.

> "The Lord God planted a garden toward the east, in Eden; and there He placed the man whom He had formed. Out of the ground the Lord God caused to grow every tree that is pleasing to the sight and good for food; the tree of life also in the midst of the garden, and the tree of knowledge of good and evil (Genesis 2:8-9)."

> Then the Lord God took the man and put him into the garden of Eden to cultivate it and keep it. The Lord God commanded the man, saying, "From any tree of the garden you may eat freely; but from the tree of knowledge of good and evil you shall not eat, for in the day that you eat from it you will surely die (Genesis 2:15-17)."

God's plan was to have a family. It still is. God's plan was to be a Father to mankind. It still is. God's plan was to be His family's source of provision for everything good. It still is. One might ask, *"What is the evil in the Tree of Knowledge of Good and Evil?"* We think of evil as the opposite of good, meaning evil as doing wrong and good is doing right. However, this Scripture was written in the original Hebrew, and those two words have a different slant. In this instance, *"good"* means *"doing what it was created to do."* *"Evil,"* in this verse, means distress, misery, and calamity! These are not what God wanted for mankind. He never intended for us to deal with stress! Stress is the number one enemy against our health today; it destroys our bodies and minds more than anything else.

Where does stress begin? In our minds! Through what does Satan work? He attacks our minds and thoughts. What did Satan cause Eve to question? God's Word. He tapped into her memory of what God had said, touched her emotions, He played on her imagination by causing her to wonder what she was missing. That is where he still works today. He cannot touch a born-again person's spirit. It is sealed unto God. The mind is the battleground. I will remind you that our physical brain controls our physical and mental wellbeing. Our brain is a physical organ that can be seen and touched physically. It causes our physical body to function. Our soul is an unseen spiritual control center for our spiritual being. Upon our physical death, our brain, as well as our body, will die. Our soul, like our spirit, is eternal and will not die.

Because our soul can be defiled, wounded, and broken, it must be healed. The only way to do that is through spiritual and emotional means. Counseling has benefits, but true restoration comes through faith in Christ Jesus. Everything we receive through Christ comes by placing our faith and confidence in Him. Being delivered from a demon or our broken soul comes through faith in Christ and allowing Holy Spirit to guide us to a life filled with truth, faith, hope, and love.

> "Therefore, I urge you, brethren, by the mercies of God, to present your bodies a living and holy sacrifice acceptable to God, which is your spiritual service of worship. And do

not be conformed to this world, but be transformed by the renewing of your mind, so that you may prove what the will of God is, that which is good and acceptable and perfect (Romans 12:1-2)."

This Scripture is clear; we must take ownership of our willingness to live holy. We cannot do this ourselves. It is by God's mercies. We must allow Holy Spirit to lead us into renewed minds. This means getting our soul in spiritual health that will align with what God has done for our spirit through salvation. This verse tells us not to conform to this world. Christ-followers' actions, thoughts, and decisions should not be driven by the world's influence. We are in this world, but we must be different.

We have three enemies—the world, ourselves, and Satan. The world's main areas of influence are education, news media, entertainment, technology, social media, and man's law, which is not founded on God's law. Of course, we, as followers of Christ, must participate in these areas so that they are influenced through us rather than us being controlled through them. It means we must renew our thinking to behave in our everyday lives to please Jesus. It means we must give up the "*I want, I think, I feel*" way of doing things. Suppose we will submit these things to Christ and align them with what God wants, thinks, and feels about all situations. In that case, we will truly walk in the principles of God's Kingdom. Doing this will produce a lifestyle of living in His power, presence, and provision!

We must stop giving our opinions and start giving God's holy instructions of righteousness. All the debating is because we want to give our opinions. We are to stick with God's righteous standard. This must be done with a clear heart and clean hands. It is not to be argued; instead, it should be stated with grace, mercy, and love. This should bring true peace even in disagreement. Remember, everyone has as much right to be wrong as anyone else. It would serve us all to remember that truth without love is brutality, and love without truth is hypocrisy. We must ensure we are stating God's truth and not our interpretation. In the following chapters, I will explain the reason for this book. Some questions that will be answered are:

1. What are spirits?
2. Why can't we see them?
3. How can Christians have demons in or attached to them?
4. If I have a demon, does that mean I am evil?
5. How do I know if I have a demon?
6. How do I get rid of a demon?
7. Even if I don't have a demon, how can I be more healed in my soul?
8. What is the difference between inner healing and deliverance?
9. Do I have to have someone else to get delivered?
10. Can I help someone else get delivered?

Notes

CHAPTER ELEVEN

Living This Life

We are in a battle whether we want it or not. I said in the previous chapter that Satan is our enemy, and his agenda is to kill, steal, and destroy. You are poorly informed or deceived if you see him as one who is just on the edge trying to mess you up. You are also deceived if you talk more about what the devil is doing in your life than how Christ is moving. Both ideas are extremes. We must understand his agenda and how he works. One must also understand God's agenda and how He works.

If you have truly accepted Christ, Satan understands he cannot take your salvation. He seeks to render you ineffective. If he can keep your spiritual growth stunted through the dysfunction of your defiled soul, he can keep you from walking in the fullness of Christ. That is what happens to most Christians. We want just enough Jesus to keep us out of hell. Let's look at the various views we have concerning the prince of darkness:

1. Satan and demons don't really exist except in abstract concepts.
2. Satan and demons are real, but they have nothing to do with me.
3. Satan and demons have no power.

4. Satan and demons are just something found in movies.
5. Satan and God are on equal footing—we won't say this, but it is how we visualize it.
6. Satan makes me do what I do, therefore, it is not my fault.

What is the truth? Let's attempt to clear up some wrong mindsets. Although God and Satan are the leading contenders for our faith, they are not equal. God is the Creator, and Satan is a created being. The created [Satan] is not and will never be more powerful than the Creator [God]. To establish truth, one must be sure of their standard. Christians say the Bible is their standard. However, too many Christians vary in their beliefs from cultural persuasions. We sometimes confuse the integrity of the Scriptures with what is taking place in society. The Bible is clear that God is love, and anything less than love is not godly. Many get confused about how this looks in our world. We are to love and accept people, but that does not mean we should embrace lifestyles outside of Scriptural perimeters.

The Bible is not merely a book of rules and regulations. It is, in fact, a history of God's interaction with mankind. It is an ever-present presentation of God revealing Himself to man. It is a guide to understanding future events of this planet and its inhabitants. The Bible is God in Word form. It is to be taken by faith and not to be understood through individual interpretation. It says what it says. We will deteriorate as a society when we endeavor to make it fit our comfort zone.

When a person receives salvation, there will be a lifestyle change, no matter if that involves their words, sexual practices, dress codes promoting wrong motives and agendas, behavior and thought altering substance abuse, and how they treat others. In other words, the pattern of one living through the "*I want, I think, I feel*" method needs to experience transformation. Remember, these three desires motivate the works of the flesh found in Galatians.

> Now the deeds of the flesh are evident, which are: sexual immorality, impurity, indecent behavior, idolatry, witchcraft, hostilities, strife, jealousy, outbursts of anger, selfish ambitions, dissensions, factions, envy, drunkenness, carousing and things like these, of which I forewarn you, just as I have forewarned you, that those who practice such things will not inherit God's Kingdom (Galatians 5: 19-21).

Take note that Scripture does not imply that a demon initiates these behavioral traits! These come from our fallen nature. The attributes listed in Galatians stem from our flesh ruled by our defiled soul, played out in our physical bodies. It also says those who practice these things will not inherit God's Kingdom. We get good at what we practice! However, we are not doomed to serving the lust of the flesh. There is complete freedom in Christ!

So where do the demons come into play? One needs only to read Romans 1, especially verses 18-32, with a desire to see the truth. The first chapter of Romans explains the wrath of God as a judgment to those who pervert God's image into anything against His holy character. In verse 24, it states that God gives them over to the lusts of their hearts to impurity. Verse 26 says God gives them over to degrading passions to change the natural use of sexual acts between men and women. Verse 28 states when people no longer see the need to acknowledge God, He gives them over to a depraved mind to do what is improper. I want to share verses 28-32 from the Complete Jewish Bible.

> In other words, since they have not considered God worth knowing, God has given them up to worthless ways of thinking, so they do improper things. They are filled with every kind of wickedness, evil, greed, and vice; stuffed with jealousy, murder, quarreling, dishonesty, and ill-will; they are gossips, slanderers, haters of God; they are insolent,

arrogant, and boastful; they plan evil schemes; they disobey their parents; they are brainless, faithless, heartless, and ruthless. They know well enough God's righteous decree that people who do such things deserve to die; yet not only do they keep doing them, but they applaud others who do the same (Romans 1: 28-32, CJB).

When we practice the works of the flesh without true repentance and the willingness to allow Holy Spirit to empower us to overcome the will of the flesh, it leads us into places we read about in Romans. Once God removes His convicting power, we become subject to demonic activity. This activity can be from within and without. Any time a person's defiled soul, which includes intellect, emotions, will, imagination, and memory, rules behaviors, we become subject to demonic interference. Deliverance and/or inner healing become necessary to get free enough to make God-inspired decisions on living by God's standards which will produce the fruit of the Spirit, as found in Galatians 5:22-23.

Notes

CHAPTER TWELVE

The Unseen Kingdom

It is difficult to deny the existence of an unseen world. We know there is a kingdom of darkness and a kingdom of light.

> "Giving thanks to the Father, who has qualified us to share in the inheritance of the saints in Light. For He rescued us from the domain of darkness and transferred us to the kingdom of His beloved son, in whom we have redemption, the forgiveness of sins (Colossians 1: 12-13).

Demonic spirits are stationed in this domain of darkness while holy angels are stationed in the Kingdom of Light. The demons [Satan's agents] and God's holy angels are spirit beings. This means they do not possess a physical body as we do. The word spirit, as seen in the Old Testament, is derived from the Hebrew word *"ruwach."* It means wind and/or breath. The New Testament Greek word for *"spirit"* is *"pneuma"* meaning *"breath."* This is one explanation for why we can't see them. Another reason we can't always see them is because they exist in a different dimension. Angels and demons are only visible to us as God allows. I have seen both multiple times, and I can assure you it is not something I take lightly, nor do I let these visuals dominate my spiritual walk. It is not wise to get caught up in looking for spirits, good or bad. Jesus warned His disciples against this.

> "Nevertheless, do not rejoice in this, that the spirits are subject to you, but rejoice that your names are recorded in heaven (Luke 10:20)."

On the question of Christians having a demon in or outside of them, spirits are all around us. Angels are commissioned by God to serve and help us.

> "Are they not all ministering spirits, sent out to provide service for the sake of those who will inherit salvation (Hebrews 1:14)."

Demons are constantly attempting to influence us to rebel against God's instructions. The demon's [evil spirit] ability to inhabit us is from sin. Remember, I talked about our broken souls. Whenever our minds, emotions, will, imagination, and memories are defiled through woundedness or defiled information, it sets a stage for demonic activity. This activity influences us without understanding how to identify and deal appropriately. Trauma also gives the enemy access to influence us from the inside. This does not make one evil.

Suppose the broken emotions and will are not dealt with properly. In that case, it enables the evil spirit to wreak havoc over our ability to allow Holy Spirit to teach us righteousness. The evil entity's power or influence must be removed for us to have the uninhibited ability to truly repent and obey Jesus Christ. Holy Spirit abides in a believer's spirit and it is sealed. The demonic takes root in our souls. It is also wise to remember a believer does not necessarily have a demon inside just because they struggle with obedience to Christ.

Demons attach themselves to the continued defilement of the soul. Whenever a believer gets saved, their behavior begins to change if they continue seeking knowledge of the Savior through the teaching of the Word, prayer, and the influence of other believers. Often, we discover that for some reason, they start drifting. They stop showing up for church, or they take up some of the habits they left behind. This may indicate something hinders them from moving forward in their faith journey. The battle to live righteously becomes overwhelming. It could be the influence of an evil presence that needs to be appropriately dealt with. This is where freedom or deliverance is necessary. It is like trying to close a door, but something is always in the way of completing the process. It could be that a demon gained access through sinful habits. It could be from trauma or a broken heart through something done to that person in their life, and it was never adequately dealt with.

We see others who seemingly live a Christian life, meaning they don't do the seen sins such as drugs, drinking alcohol, cussing, cheating, or all the things we consider the *"big stuff."* However, they don't really exhibit Christ-like qualities. We see them gossiping, talking about the preacher, trying to run the church according to their rules, and a plethora of other things. This may be from their lack of discipline, but we must wonder, why is there such a lack? I realize this possibly will require something that makes church leaders nervous. Confrontation! At any rate, it is time to get serious about kicking the devil out of the church and become the powerful entity Christ desires to claim as His bride upon His return. He is not returning for a sin-stained girlfriend but a glorious bride without spots, wrinkles, or blemishes.

> …Christ also loved the church and gave Himself up for her, so that He might sanctify her, having cleansed her by the washing of water with the word, that He might present to Himself the church in all her glory, having no spot or wrinkle or any such thing but that she would be holy and blameless (Ephesians 25-27).

This has always been important but never like it is today. We see our society and world crumbling around us. Good is being called evil, and evil is being presented as good. Much of the Church is unsure of the boundaries between right and wrong. We have allowed the culture and the need to be men-pleasers to draw our lines of righteousness. The Church is supposed to be a guiding force of righteousness on the Earth, yet we have allowed the world to define our beliefs. It is time to get back to the integrity of God's Word. We are to embrace people but not lifestyles of unrighteousness. We always hear, *"Well, we have to love everyone."* This is true; however, true love appropriately confronts sin, gives solutions, and helps walk through difficulties to freedom.

There is a problem with pastors not knowing how to address cultural situations. Many situations pressing in our churches are ignored through fear or ignorance of how to properly deal with them. I have pastors reaching out to me to deal with young people who believe they are transgender because they don't know how to address it or don't have time to invest. This is why we need the entire church body equipped to help others walk in true fellowship with Holy Spirit! Who will restrain evil on the Earth when the Church no longer looks any different than the world?

We are called to be ambassadors who bring men into reconciliation with God. God is holy and will not tolerate darkness. Holiness is not up for man's interpretation! It is clearly defined in God's Word and must once again become our standard. I'm not talking about legalism or judgmentalism of anyone who doesn't look like us. The days are getting darker, and we, as followers of Christ, need to be as spiritually healthy as possible to stand in the evil day. I am not a doomsday preacher, but I believe our days are quickly coming to a climax. We must ensure nothing hinders us from walking in the light to lead others to the truth. What we believe means nothing if it is not in proper alignment with the standard of truth, which is the person Jesus Christ.

When people endeavor to find happiness by pursuing what they want, ruling their lives by how they feel, believing what they think, and finding it leaves them empty and hopeless, they will need somewhere to run for help. The Church may discover a whole new generation at its door. Will we be equipped and willing to invest to bring them out of darkness into the glorious light of salvation? Only if we are sure of what we believe and can walk it out in genuine faith, hope, and love without hindrances of our own darkened souls. We can only take someone where we are.

Come on, Church, let's get healed from past hurts and failures and become leaders of righteousness. Let's follow the simple outlines defined in the following chapters to become as free as possible and then do what we can to help others. The lost depend on us to show the true way to salvation and deliverance from a perverse generation.

> "Do all things without complaining and arguments; so that you will prove yourselves to be blameless and innocent, children of God above reproach in the midst of a crooked and perverse generation, among whom you appear as lights in the world… (Philippians 2:14-15)."

Notes

CHAPTER THIRTEEN

Where Do I Begin?

Inner healing is like everything else. It is a choice. I want to be clear—there are traumas people experience that are, at best, difficult to overcome. Some traumas leave one so damaged it may always leave a lasting effect on their life. That said, nothing is too tricky for Christ. As someone who might help bring inner healing, I realize I may have limits in severe cases. It is essential to know when to call in other resources. In deliverance or inner healing, you must understand your limitations and set appropriate boundaries.

A good rule of thumb is you must never want freedom for someone more than they want it for themselves. Holy Spirit will never violate someone's will, nor should we. Deliverance is not a magic wand, nor something we do to someone. The body of Christ is coming alongside a brother or sister to stand in support and agreement for their freedom. We are to guide the process, not control the person. We have authority over evil spirits, not people. We must never violate a person's will even if it leaves them in the same state as they came. It is wise to know deliverance, inner healing, or any change in one's life does not stop at the event, but it takes walking it out daily. We may have to learn new habits and how to renew our thinking. This is why discipleship is so essential. I like to address it as prayer ministry. We may have to address a demon occasionally, but our focus should remain on the Lord. Prayer is how we communicate with the Lord and listen for instruction through Holy Spirit.

One of the significant turning points in deliverance for me came as I sought the Lord on how to do it more effectively. The Lord took me to a story in Mark 9. Apparently, the disciples of Christ had been asked to get a demon out of a boy and could not do it. Jesus had just come from the mountain of transfiguration. When the man approached Jesus to help him, the boy's father recounted how the boy could not speak from a spirit; the spirit would slam him to the ground and cause him to foam at the mouth, grind his teeth, and become stiff. If you ever saw someone have an epileptic seizure, it would look like this.

> And they brought the boy to Him. When he saw Him, the spirit immediately threw him into convulsions, and falling to the ground, he began rolling around and foaming at the mouth. And He asked his father, "How long has this been happening to him?" and he said, From childhood. It has often thrown him both into the fire and into the water to kill him but if You can do anything, take pity on us and help us!" But Jesus said to him, "'If You can?' All things are possible for the one who believes." Immediately the boy's father cried out and said, "I do believe; help my unbelief!" When Jesus saw that a crowd was rapidly gathering, He rebuked the unclean spirit, saying to it, "You mute and deaf spirit, I command you, come out of him and do not enter him again!" And after crying out and throwing him into terrible convulsions, it came out; and the boy became so much like a corpse that most of them said, "He is dead!" But Jesus took him by the hand and raised him and he got up. When He came into the house, His disciples began asking Him privately, "Why is it that we could not cast it out?" And He said to them, "This

kind cannot come out by anything except prayer (Mark 9: 20-29).

In the Kings James Version, the last verse says, *"This kind can come forth by nothing but prayer and fasting."* Many truths are hidden in this account that ensure deliverance success. For now, I want to share the one thing that changed my perspective concerning this type of ministry. When Jesus appeared on the scene, the evil spirit convulsed the boy. This young man was rolling on the ground and foaming at the mouth. What did Jesus do? Did He immediately tell the demon to stop or even cast him out of the boy? No! Jesus turns and starts a conversation with the boy's father! Holy Spirit had me read this repeatedly until it finally dawned on me what He was trying to get me to see. We know because of who Jesus is. He already knew how long this boy had been in this condition.

As I continued to listen to Holy Spirit giving me insight into what He wanted me to see, I finally got it! Again, if you can picture the intensity of this situation, a boy, perhaps in his teens, because his father told Jesus he had been that way since childhood, rolling on the ground and foaming at the mouth. Instead of demanding the spirit controlling this helpless boy to stop, He turns and casually talks to the father. I was about to learn a life-changing lesson. What Holy Spirit revealed to me was eye-opening. Jesus was letting the boy's father know that He recognized this situation had cost him. Perhaps He was conveying He knew his heartache. The shame and loss had been challenging. There was no reason for Jesus to take the time to ask a question to which He already knew the answer. As I reread this portion, Holy Spirit said to me, *"Remember this, Sandy, you are not ministering to demons. You are ministering to human beings. You deal with the spirit as I give you instructions. Still, your job in deliverance is to bring that person out as whole as possible with dignity, love, and respect."*

That was the purpose of Jesus talking to the father, to show He was aware of the problems the situation had caused him. Jesus was restoring the father as well as the son! This is the purpose of deliverance ministry, or any ministry, to restore a person to a place where they can walk in fellowship with their Creator without hindrance. Too often, we focus on the demonic activity, not the person we minister to.

> Now the seventy-two returned with joy saying, "Lord, even the demons are subject to us in Your name!" And He said to them, "I watched Satan fall from heaven like lightning. Behold, I have given you authority to walk on snakes and scorpions, and authority over all the power of the enemy, and nothing will injure you. "Nevertheless, do not rejoice in this, that the spirits are subject to you, but rejoice that your names are recorded in heaven (Luke 10:18)."

Notes

CHAPTER FOURTEEN

Who Is Qualified?

One might ask, *"Is deliverance ministry necessary considering Jesus completed victory over darkness on the cross?"* I covered in the earlier chapters several accounts of demonic activity within people. Even after Jesus died, resurrected, and ascended to the Father, we see the Apostle Paul dealing with demonic spirits inside of people. There are multiple accounts of demonic activity through people in the Bible. If demonic spirits within people were eliminated at the cross, how do you explain the extreme scenarios we see unfolding today? Yes, succumbing to a life of sin will exhibit darkness, but if it was removed from the table because of the work on the cross, why would Jesus have left instructions for the disciples to cast out demons? If that stopped at the death of the last apostle, do you really believe Jesus would allow the demonic to have such power over humans without the body of Christ having spiritual recourse?

This book is not about proving the presence of demons in people, although through the Scriptures, that has been made clear. Ask any minister if they have seen people who say they know Christ as Savior but never seem to overcome the darkness in their faith journey. If all has been done through prayer, studying Scripture, and instructions of righteousness, and still there is something that hinders a Christ-follower from walking in victory, then one must wonder why.

We are the body of Christ, meaning we are extensions of His work on Earth. We are to continue what He modeled before us while on this planet. He alone can destroy the power of Satan, but we are instructed to be teachers of righteousness. Satan is still at work through deception, lies, and influencing the hearts of men. Our job is to expose and break the connection of that darkness through the ministry of reconciliation. Sometimes that includes evicting an illegal resident through inner healing and/or deliverance. So, who is qualified to do this ministry? Any born-again believer in Jesus Christ. However, before going into deliverance, there must be some level of maturity and instruction, as with any ministry. Some will be more adaptable than others, as the Scripture clarifies that only some do the same ministry. However, it is a believer's responsibility to help brothers and sisters in Christ to walk in the light with victory.

> "But the goal of our instruction is love from a pure heart, from a good conscience, and from a sincere faith (1 Timothy 1:5)."

> "The things which you have heard from me in the presence of many witnesses, entrust these to faithful people who will be able to teach others also (2 Timothy 2:2)."

> "No soldier in active service entangles himself in the affairs of everyday life, so that he may please the one who enlisted him. And if someone likewise competes as an athlete he is not crowned as victor unless he competes according to the rules (2 Timothy 2:4-5)."

> "Giving thanks to the Father, who has qualified us to share in the inheritance of the saints in light (Colossians 1:12)."

Every believer should be willing to submit themselves to believers proven to be mature in faith, endeavoring to maintain a pure heart, keeping a good conscience, and living in faith consistent with Scripture; a person who does not get tangled in life's controversies but keeps their eyes on what pleases God. We must be willing to declare the teachings of Scripture and not determine truth by our opinions or culture. Going through a session of confessing one's faults to another person found faithful in living as described above can be beneficial in living to the fullest. This also enables one to take others through effective prayer ministry to eradicate the residue of sinful behavior.

Why is this so important now? It has always been true, however, as we see the day of Christ's return so much clearer, we know that the darkness is getting intense from the times we live in. As the Scriptures clearly define, the times where evil is called good and good is called evil, we need more than ever to be free from anything that might give the enemy a foothold to sway us from seeing the truth.

> "I will not speak much more with you, for the ruler of the world is coming and he has nothing in regard to Me (John 14:30)."

Jesus talked to some of His disciples and told them He was preparing to go to the cross. He was going to be cautious talking about it and explaining that the enemy had nothing to accuse Him. Sometimes we talk too much! Jesus was declaring there is nothing in Him defiled or broken onto which the enemy to grasp hold. Even though He is all God, He also was a man of flesh. He knew the flesh could become a stumbling block, so He kept Himself pure from the entanglements of this human life.

We are of the flesh. We are not God, even on our best days! We do have defilements of sin's residue. Our sin, if confessed and repented through faith in Christ, is totally forgiven, and we are born-again. However, our soul is not redeemed because Romans 12:2 tells us we must be transformed by renewing our minds to not think the way the world thinks. This defilement is a place where Satan has access. The Scriptures are clear about how we must constantly die to ourselves to live in God's Spirit.

Let me pull this together and bring home the point. If as a spiritual leader, pastor, or one who has a strong influence in other's lives and after reading this book, you see the value of implementing an inner healing/deliverance ministry as part of your curriculum, it is essential for you to take the following action.

If you are interested in establishing this type of ministry and want to do it under the umbrella of your church, you must go to your pastor and get their cooperation. Whether you do this within the church or independently, the basic rules of operation are the same. If you are the pastor of a local body interested in further information, I will be glad to do hands-on training.

The first thing is prayer. Seek God and get His guidance on how this would benefit your setting. Ask Holy Spirit to show several people within your church or close circles who exhibit spiritual maturity. You probably already have an idea of who these people might be. Pay attention to how these people handle their relationships, finances, and emotions and how effectively they interact with others. I suggest starting out with a small group, and as you mature in this ministry, you will find others prepared to join.

Next, spend time with this group in prayer. You must get familiar with and grow in trust with each other. Integrity is an absolute must! Creating a safe place for others to divulge their darkest thoughts and deeds is imperative. During deliverance, you will be exposed to people's pain, secrets, and darkest emotions. Hidden sins will be revealed. Personal information will be given, and you must know how to properly deal with that without being judgmental and keep it within the ministry team. This is why it is crucial to whom you allow to minister deliverance. If you deal with prejudices against any particular people group or specific dysfunctions within society—drug abusers, homosexuals, adulterers, people of color, or a race different than yours, you need to experience deliverance and walk that out before you deal with others. I find this helpful when instructing others: think of what you consider the worst of society's offenders or what you consider the worst of the worst sin. If you cannot see yourself ministering to that person with true love, compassion, and a deep desire to see them free without prejudice, and condemnation, you should seek and receive inner healing. It is a good idea to undergo some deliverance and inner healing before moving into a deliverance ministry. Besides, it is an excellent way to practice! I go through this process often because if I am not willing to examine myself and keep myself from the world's defilement, why would I expect others to trust me?

One of the main things you will need to grow in is spiritual discernment. Having a structured format and guide to use during deliverance is good. You must keep in mind you are dealing with spirits, and we, in our natural understanding, are not equipped to see what is beyond the information we are getting from a human being. Never go into a session with the thoughts of your experience or know-how as your guide. Your dependence must be on the ministry of Holy Spirit. How do you get spiritual discernment? Some think they are discerning when they are only operating in suspicion. We can sense when we are being told the truth or not being told the whole story by watching human behavior. This is okay, but that is not enough in dealing with supernatural beings. There are two ways to obtain spiritual discernment. Both are found in the Bible.

> For though by this time, you ought to be teachers, you have need again for someone to teach you the elementary principles of the actual words of God, and you have come to need milk and not solid food. For everyone who partakes

> only of milk is unacquainted with the word of righteousness, for he is an infant. But solid food is for the mature, who because of practice have their senses trained to distinguish between good and evil (Hebrews 5:12-14).

We see in this portion of Scripture that discernment is a skill obtained through knowing and applying God's Word. There is another way in which to have discernment of spirits.

> But to each one is given the manifestation of the Spirit for the common good. For to one is given the word of wisdom through the Spirit, and to another the word of knowledge according to the same Spirit; to another faith by the same Spirit, and to another gifts of healing by the one Spirit, and to the effecting of miracles, and to another prophecy, and to another the **distinguishing of spirits,** to another various kinds of tongues, and to another the interpretation of tongues. But one and the same Spirit works all these things, distributing to each one individual just as He wills (1 Corinthians 12:7-11).

This is clearly defined as a gift of Holy Spirit and is given to members of the body of Christ as He sees fit. This is a supernatural occurrence and is not owned by humans. One last thought before we move on. Again, I want to clarify that salvation is through Christ alone and not through anything we can do except receive this gift by faith. That is the only way to heaven. The blood of Christ applied is the only assurance of salvation. Deliverance and/or inner healing is so the believer can be free of any left-over residue of sin we may have practiced, which leaves an influence within our soul. A demon cannot enter the spirit of someone who has given their life to Christ! Deliverance and/or inner healing is another tool to help the believer effectively walk out of this faith journey.

Notes

CHAPTER FIFTEEN

Getting Prepared

As the deliverance team prepares for a ministry session, a few things need to be settled. Who, when, and where? I suggest two people minister; a third is fine so long as one of the members agrees to stay in the background to watch, learn, and pray. Having too many listening to their story can be overwhelming for the one receiving ministry. The deliverance recipient [receiver] should only have someone accompany them if they are a minor, which we will cover later. Ensure everyone knows when to be there and allow at least two hours for the first session. Where this ministry transpires is important. It needs to be private, comfortable, and free from any interference. It is best to have a place conditioned with prayer. At least know the environment. You don't want to go where sin has full reign. You will come against agents of darkness, so you want to set an atmosphere conducive to success. Do not fear. You have angels of light, the power of God, and the word of truth as your protection!

On the day of deliverance, each participant needs to be on time, dressed comfortably, and all cell phones turned off. The focus needs to be on the ministry at hand without distractions. You will need a few things: paper, pencils or pens, tissues, and water. It is best not to have food as it can be a distraction. Everyone should eat a light meal or snack beforehand. It is best to have chairs rather than a sofa. The chairs must be positioned so the recipient will face team members. You will need a small waste basket lined with a plastic bag for dirty tissues; sometimes, the person being delivered will feel a need to spit out something and/or vomit. This is common, and often it represents getting rid of something spiritual or emotional. Usually, it takes several sessions to complete a deliverance. Remember, they didn't get into this place overnight, and they may need more time than a couple of hours.

Decide beforehand who will be the primary facilitator. Another member will need to take notes. As the receiver talks, you will hear information that may need to be questioned or addressed. Every team member needs to always stay alert and attentive. You must be watchful of attitudes, body postures, facial expressions, and signs of physical distresses. It is advisable to ask all team members and the receiver to avoid walking around during sessions since it can be a distraction. No matter what you hear, never show disgust or shock. This needs to be a safe place for the person to reveal whatever is necessary for freedom.

Before starting:

1. have a short conversation
2. introduce yourselves
3. try to give positive assurance of a good outcome
4. tell the receiver what to expect

Think of it as a visit to a medical doctor. Ask the receiver what they hope to accomplish and what their issues are. Even though you will have some information on the forms, it is more personal to have dialog. As a warning, you may have to rein the person in from nervousness, personality, and/or spiritual interference. The ministry receiver can hijack the session by talking incessantly. Evil spirits will try to control the session if they are active. You must be discerning. Members of the prayer team must refrain from too much dialog.

If a child receives ministry, it is best to have someone with experience in this type ministry. The questions should be kept age appropriate and simple. Most likely, the questions will be geared toward behaviors of which the parents have expressed concerns. Be careful that nothing is implied, which might lead the child to confess something untrue. Just allow the child to tell their story naturally. Ask Holy Spirit to lead you to address the two or three primary issues. You are dealing with a child; it is best to keep it simple. Remember, there are no little demons, and more importantly, no little Holy Spirit! I strongly urge a parent or guardian to be present but ask them to stay out of the way and quiet. You don't want their emotions to interfere.

It is essential to always be mindful of boundaries. If there are traumas you are not prepared to deal with, you may have to suggest professional care. You are not a psychiatrist or a medical doctor. You are dealing with spiritual defilements. You will understand this more as you review the outline of deliverance steps. This is also why having a pastor connected to this ministry is necessary. If there are legal implications, you may need their guidance. An example might be a confession of sexual assault, child abuse, or illegal activity.

Team members should be free from judgments, personal opinions, and the need to promote shame and condemnation. You will hear confessions of perhaps adultery, sexual misconduct, violence, perverse desires, and other things you may feel strongly about. I have dealt with pedophiles (not active, but in their past served time in prison and have given their life to Christ), same-sex attractions, rape victims, all sorts of sexual sins as well as dysfunctions within the home, and those who have had abortions. Our job is not to fix or judge anyone but to help them come to freedom from shame, guilt, and fear, which keeps them in bondage. We are to help restore the soul to a place where they can implement better behaviors to walk out their faith journey more effectively.

Deliverance and/or inner healing is simply a process of helping others reach a place where there is a receiving of truth and releasing of anything that has caused them to have damaged emotions, stubborn and unsubmitted wills toward God, prideful intelligence that blocks genuine humility, a defiled imagination, and compromised memories which keep them locked in the failures of yesterday and repeating sins. Implementation will vary depending on the person needing freedom, the ministry teams' approach, and the depth of the wounds within the soul. However, there are basic rules one should follow, and I will give an outline. As a leader grows in knowledge and understanding of how to be led by Holy Spirit in this ministry, the format may look different. Still, the outline of steps is an excellent way to discover the necessary information to obtain a good outcome.

It is best if you are going to make yourself available to participate in deliverance ministry to stay in an attitude of prayer and learning to hear Holy Spirit's voice to the point you know His voice as well as your own. It is important to have at least a couple of experienced people in this area to lend advice and stay connected for guidance. It is not a one-man- show. You also must grow in the area of humility and holy boldness. Your confidence must be centered in Christ. The minute you start depending on your experience alone, you must take a break and reconnect with Christ. It is a spiritual battle for which we are not equipped within ourselves.

Notes

CHAPTER SIXTEEN

Why Deliverance?

There are many levels of deliverance, and some of them can get very deep in dealing with intense darkness. Holy Spirit directed me to keep this book simple with basic instructions. A few areas may require more intense ministry, such as the occult, sexual disorders, cults, addictions, and deep trauma.

> But we have this treasure in earthen containers, so that the extraordinary greatness of the power will be of God and not from ourselves; we are afflicted in every way, but not crushed; perplexed, but not despairing; persecuted, but not abandoned; struck down, but not destroyed; always carrying around in the body the dying of Jesus, so that the life of Jesus may also be revealed in our body. For we who live are constantly being handed over to death because of Jesus, so that the life of Jesus may also be revealed in our mortal flesh (2 Corinthians 4:7-11).

There are three distinct areas of needed deliverances:

1. **Salvation**: Salvation is a deliverance of its own. Before anything can be done on a spiritual level, one must be born-

again. It is Christ alone who has the power to deliver us from the penalty of sin. Christ delivers us from the kingdom of darkness into His marvelous light. We have no power over darkness when we are a participant of darkness (2 Thessalonians 1:8-9).

2. **Obedience**: Once a person is born-again, spiritual growth should be evident. When a true believer does not exhibit a continued separation from works of the flesh found in Galatians 5:19-21 and actively developing the fruit of the Spirit, there may be a blockage in the maturing process. It would be beneficial to find out what that blockage is. There are probably soul wounds that need inner healing and if there are dark spirits attached, then get rid of them. Usually believers who admit they are lacking in something will often tell you what the problem is. For example, they may say something like, *"I can't get over this anger,"* or *"I can't seem to move past my grief,"* or *"I constantly worry,"* or *"I just can't forgive them."* A believer's issues will usually have to do with unresolved emotions. Often the *"I want, I feel, I think"* of their unhealed soul rules their behavior. These exhibit the ruling of the person's old nature. Going through the steps presented in the last chapters will be helpful in walking out obedience and on to victory.

3. **Demon Activity**: This is the part we as Christians don't want to believe and/or deal with. Don't make it harder than it must be. If there is demonic activity within a person's behavior, the acknowledgement does not show weakness but spiritual maturity to want freedom! Again, it is about the choice to be free or stay in bondage. When a person has lived in total rebellion, drug addiction, or any lifestyle demanding a life outside Christ, chances are, there will be some demonic attachments. Once they accept Christ, it is not uncommon for instant deliverance to occur, but sometimes it takes other

steps to ensure freedom to walk in victory. Any person who has accepted Christ as Savior will go to heaven when they die or He returns, if they stay the course. Deliverance is about getting freedom from anything that hinders a life of peace, joy and fullness of Holy Spirit power.

Deliverance, inner healing, and/or prayer ministry is nothing less than coming alongside another believer with attachments of darkness embedded in their defiled souls. Through this ministry of guidance, instruction, repentance, and agreement with righteousness, deception will be exposed so that the life of Christ can be more intensely revealed.

The Bible speaks of demonic spirits, from which many defilements flow through our participation throughout our life. If a person has received Christ, they are forgiven and Christian. I continually state this to remain clear about Christ's complete work. Deliverance ministry helps expose the influence these entities hold against the soul. Through repentance, forgiveness, and renouncing the works of darkness, a person can let go of strongholds that keep them from walking in freedom. These are spirits named in the Bible. Some of the following information in this list came from *Strongman's His Name…What's His Game* by Drs Jerry and Carol Robeson. Underneath are influences that fall under their territories:

1. **Spirit of Divination**: (Acts 16:16-18) rebellion, fortune telling, witchcraft, astrology, magic, drugs (Greek word, pharmakos, from where we get our word pharmacy.)
2. **Familiar Spirit**: (Leviticus 19:31) like the spirit of divination, it involves receiving information from the spiritual realm from an evil spirit. It involves mediums, palm readers, tarot cards, crystal balls, yoga (not just an exercise, look up its origin), or any such item where information from the spirit realm outside of Holy Spirit is gathered. Any participation of Ouija

boards, horoscopes, spirit guides or any type of communing with the dead needs to be repented. Movies or video games that promote darkness, vampires, murder, violence, sexual content should not be in anyone's entertainment lineup. Parents must guard the music allowed in their home. Stop buying tickets to concerts that promote ungodly lifestyles!

3. **Spirit or Attitude of Jealousy**: (Numbers 5:14) anger, rage, envy, revenge or spite, hatred, murder, extreme competition (extreme emotion or anger when a particular team wins or loses is an example.) Again, parents should be cautioned in promoting the need to keep their children in material gain to keep up with others.

4. **Lying or Deceiving Spirit**: (2 Chronicles 18:22) strong deception, flattery, superstitions, slander, gossip, accusations, religious bondages (believing their experiences over God's Word), little white lies, exaggeration.

5. **Perverse or Spirit of Distortion**: (Isaiah 19:14) twisting of truth, twisting, or perverting Word of God, pornography, atheist, filthy mind, chronic worrier, incest, evil actions, child abuse, abortion, doctrinal error.

6. **Spirit of Haughtiness or Pride**: (Proverbs 16:18) arrogance, self-righteousness, laziness, habitual laziness, believing you are always right, or you aways have information no one else has, rebellion (especially against authority) Pride takes on many faces, someone who is always apologizing, or declaring they are not worthy of Christ, this is false humility and a form of pride. Pride always says, *"Look at me!"* controlling, manipulative. Habitual lateness (this also can be connected to control.)

7. **Spirit or Heaviness or a Disheartened Spirit**: (Isaiah 61: 3) excessive grief, self-pity, broken heart, suicidal thoughts, inner hurts, depression, anxiety, stress, feelings of rejection,

despair, hopelessness, emotional disorders, unexplained feelings of sadness or stress.
8. **Spirit of Infidelity**: (Hosea 5:4) lust, unfaithfulness/adultery, fornication, multiple sex partners, excessive appetite, idolatry, spirit, soul and/or body prostitution, chronic dissatisfaction.
9. **Spirit of Infirmity or Sickness**: (Luke 13:11-13) lingering disorders, cancer, arthritis, asthma, allergies, physical ailments of which you cannot find a cause, always sick with one thing or another.
10. **Deaf and Dumb or Mute Spirit**: (Mark 9:17-29) unable to speak, constant crying, ear problems, seizures, mental illness, blindness (spiritual, unable to see truth), suicidal.
11. **Spirit of Bondage or Slavery**: (Romans 8:15) fears, addictions (tobacco, drugs, marijuana, alcohol, food, sex, video games, gossip) compulsive sin (this may include a person who cannot make Godly decisions) fear of death, fear of being alone. Hoarding. Excessive exercise or competition. Obsession with body weight. These last two also involve pride.
12. **Spirit of Fear or Timidity**: (2 Timothy 1:7) fears, phobias, heart attacks, fear of man (worry of what others might think) anxiety, stress, untrusting, tormenting dreams, nightmares, fear of death, extreme shyness. Obsession with weight. Hoarding. Poverty mindset.
13. **Seducing or Deceitful Spirits**: (1 Timothy 4:1) fascination with prophets and/or the prophetic, miracles, signs, and wonders (unable to walk in obedience to Christ but always consumed with the supernatural) constantly running to conferences and seminars for the sake of getting in the next move of God, always looking for other's revelation and never getting any from Holy Spirit themselves. Note: there is nothing wrong with listening to others who have insight on what God is doing, but the problem comes when one has

difficulty living out their Christian faith in everyday life but always fascinated with what others know. Being drawn to the dark side of the supernatural (books, music, movies, games), wandering from the truth.

14. **Spirit of Anti-Christ**: (1 John4:3) denies deity of Christ, against Christ and His teachings, denies atonement of Christ, new revelations that cannot consistently be based in Scriptures, humanism, lawlessness, anti-Christian, teachers of heresies, worldly speech, and actions, denying any part of the New Testament teachings as being part of the church doctrine. Denying any part of the Word (Christ was the Word made flesh, to deny the Word is to deny Christ, (John 1:1 & 14) idolatry of any kind.
15. **Spirit of Error**: (1 John 4:6) un-submissive to authority especially sound spiritual authority, unteachable, New Age movement, defensiveness, argumentative, defends God's revelation to them personally without validation in Scripture, false doctrine, corrupt living, corrupt speech, twisting Scripture to validate doctrine, denomination, or way of life.

Personality traits to be aware of might indicate strong holds:

1. **Anger**: unresolved anger or easily offended, feelings of no one being able to do things right except you, resentment, frustration, jealousy.
2. **Control**: Do you feel you are the only one who can do it right? Do you feel you can lead better than anyone else? Must you always have to have the last say or word? The need to speak for others. Control is really insecurity, the need to be needed, and pride colliding! Do you find yourself thinking or even saying, *"I would have done that differently."* Continued lateness. This is pride and control.

3. **Insecurity**: This is a feeling of not measuring up or the fear someone is not going to like, love or accept you. Fear of disappointment. Feeling unworthy. This can also indicate false humility which is a form of pride. It would sound like this, *"I'm not worthy to do this for God."*
4. **Guilt and/or shame**: Keeps you stuck in the past. Keeps you from doing the things necessary to move forward in life and relationships. Unworthiness. Remember: Christ did not die to make us worthy, He died to show us our worth to the Father!
5. **Sexual sin:** anything outside of God's divine order. Sex was designed by God to procreate, bring unity and fulfill physical desires under the covenant of marriage. Anything which violates His holy perspective is a breaking of His divine order. We are dealing with an influx of sexual reassignments. This is against God's divine order. It is a perversion, it must be dealt with as such but with love, mercy and grace. Sexual confusion of any kind is a trick of Satan to pervert God's order. The church at large must take a definite stand and not be swayed by the culture.
6. **Unforgiveness**: this is paramount against the ability to walk in freedom! Forgiveness is the foundation for anything spiritual to operate properly. This is because it was the complete basis for Christ to be on a cross! Without it we cannot experience God and without walking in forgiveness it is impossible to walk in right fellowship with others. Unity will never happen until we lay ourselves down in the need to be right. Forgiving others and ourselves is the key to spiritual freedom. You will hear this during deliverance, *"I just cannot forgive them, or I can forgive so and so but I cannot forgive myself!"*

Alexander Pope of the 18th century said, *"To err is human, to forgive is divine."* He was correct. We are not capable of forgiveness within our human nature. God is the author and giver of forgiveness; forgiveness can only come through us as a movement of God's Spirit. Forgiveness is a choice to allow God to flow through us. Choice is a human allowing either God or Satan to flow through. God will always encourage righteousness. Remember, while on the cross, Jesus said, "*Father, forgive them, for they do not know what they are doing* (Luke 23:34)."

We are clueless about the devastation unforgiveness brings into our lives. The burden of forgiveness is on Christ. The burden to allow Him to bring it is on us. Choose wisely. Everything we receive from Christ is through choice! He forces nothing on us. You choose God; He will bring it to pass if you stay the course.

Sanctification has been lost in the church. It simply means to be set apart. It is about becoming spiritually mature through repentance and continued growth, receiving, and walking out the truth in obedience without excuse. The last chapters will give an outline form of deliverance. I leave you with the words of the Apostle Paul.

> For this reason, I too, having heard of the faith in the Lord Jesus which exists among you and your love for all the saints, do not cease giving thanks for you, while making mention of you in my prayers; that the God of our Lord Jesus Christ, the Father of glory, may give you a spirit of wisdom and of revelation in the knowledge of Him. I pray that the eyes of your heart may be enlightened, so that you will know what is the hope of His calling, what are the riches of the glory of His inheritance in the saints, and what the boundless greatness of His power toward us who believe. These are in accordance with the working of the strength of His might which He brought about in Christ, when He raised Him from the dead and seated Him at His right hand in the heavenly places, far above all rule and authority and power and dominion, and every name that is named, not only in

this age but also in the one to come. And He put all things in subjection under His feet and made Him head over all things to the church, which is His body, the fulness of Him who fills all in all (Ephesians 1:15-23).

Notes

CHAPTER SEVENTEEN

What To Look For

Satan looks for a foothold in which to establish his agenda to kill, steal, and destroy. His main agenda in a believer of Jesus Christ is to render their testimony ineffective.

> "In your anger do not sin: Do not let the sun go down while you are still angry. And do not give the devil a foothold (Ephesians 4: 26-27, NIV)."

The King James version replaces foothold with place, and other versions replace foothold with opportunity. No matter, it all means the same. "*Foothold*" means a secure place of advancement. Anger at something or someone is often the root of many defilements. It must be repented and disengaged from the soul. Footholds often occur when the hurts of life are not adequately dealt with. This is a list of footholds the enemy uses for advancement:

1. **Continuous Sin**: Sins or habits you tend to repeat and cannot seem to overcome
2. **Unforgiveness**: Forgiveness often comes in layers. If you find yourself saying or thinking, "I forgive them but…" "I'll

forgive them if…" or "I'll forgive them when…" you need to again choose forgiveness.
3. **Addictions**: Anything keeping you involved in time, energy, resources, or money you don't or shouldn't give. Anything interfering with keeping you from developing right relationships with God or family.
4. **Traumas**: Anything that has caused you great shame or embarrassment that hinders you from functioning normally in life.
5. **Involvement With False Religions**: Any religious beliefs that require you to promote yourself as being good enough. Any religion that requires you to follow a person or their rules. If Christ alone is not the focus, you may be involved with a false religion.
6. **Fears/Phobias**: Anything that causes an interruption of normal behavior. An unnatural concern that rules behavior.
7. **Immorality**: Any actions, habits, or behaviors outside of godly parameters.
8. **Pornography**: Any picture, movies, books, media, speech, conversations, images that excite sexual desire, placing an unrealistic expectation for sexual gratification.
9. **Occultic Involvement**: One of the definitions of *"occult"* is *"hidden or concealed,"* ultimately it is a desire for knowledge beyond one's natural ability to learn. It is a desire to obtain information from a source outside of God's permission. Desiring to get information through mediums, horoscopes, games that unlock supernatural beings or knowledge. Communication with spirits, worshipping demonic beings. Palm reading and psychic readings are among many occultic practices. Movies and videos that promote dark arts, spirit guides, witches, warlocks, vampires, magic, or humans turning into animals should not be a part of your life. Concerts that do not express godly views or lifestyles can be occultic in

nature. Even chasing after angels or following supernatural events on a Christian level just to be in a supernatural realm can become out of order. God wants and does communicate with us, but be wary if signs, wonders, and miracles take the place of spiritual growth through true fellowship with God and His people. Spiritual information should be obtained through studying God's Word for balance and faithful spiritual growth. The gifts of the Holy Spriit should always point you into a closer walk with the Lord while exhibiting fruit of the Spirit.

10. **Sexual Sins**: Any sexual behaviors outside of God's parameters. Also, be careful about allowing unhealthy and ungodly thoughts freedom to run amuck. Lusting after someone in your mind needs to be dealt with.
11. **Word Curses/ Negative Words Toward Self And Others**: Guard your words, they have great influence.
12. **Ungodly Or Unhealthy Soul Ties**: Influences through a tie that is formed through relationships.
13. **Faulty Belief Systems**: Anything that puts an unrealistic burden on you.

To be clear, Jesus paid the total price with His blood to purchase our freedom from the penalty of sin. The residue remains, and through repentance and the empowerment of Holy Spirit, we have a responsibility to rid our souls of these defilements. They may not keep us from heaven, but they will keep us from the fullness of an abundant life of freedom. Seven areas need to be addressed that may contribute to a foothold. Jesus broke the curse; however, the residue of generational sin can be passed down much like spiritual DNA:

1. **Generational Sins and Curses**: Attributes of sin passed through family lines. We see this exhibited in multi-

WHAT TO LOOK FOR

generations of alcohol or drug addictions, diseases (heart, diabetes arthritis, female reproductive disorders etc.), divorce, and any trait seen repeated within a family. It could be learned behavior and spiritual influences as well. The root needs to be addressed.

2. **Ungodly Soul Ties:** Ties are formed through relationships which influence our decisions and behaviors. Soul ties are like invisible power lines between two people, places or things where emotional information is exchanged. These form strong ties that bind. These can be healthy as well as unhealthy and even ungodly ties between people. An example of being tied to a place may be someone believing they can only be happy living in a certain area. Some biblical examples are:

"After David had finished talking with Saul, Jonathan became one in spirit with David, and he loved him as himself (1 Samuel 18:1)."

In 2 Samuel 13, the story of Amnon, David's son, fell in love with his sister, Tamar. Amnon was said to be sick because he wanted her, knowing it was wrong for him to have her. Amnon tricked Tamar into coming to his room, pretending to be sick. Long story short, he raped her, and once he did, he despised her. She felt tied to him because she had been a virgin and begged him to keep her. She was a reminder of his sin; he put her out, and she was devastated. This is an example of an ungodly and unhealthy soul tie.

"Or do you not know that the one who joins himself to a prostitute is one body with her? For He says, *'THE TWO SHALL BECOME ONE FLESH* (1 Corinthians 6:16).'"

Strong soul ties are created through childbirth between parents and children, any sexual unions, whenever sinful behavior is shared, such as drug use, violence, cult activity, being in a group, military, sororities, or any activity that declares allegiance to another. These form soul ties, strong bonds that negatively influence how they look at life unless broken and renounced.

3. **False Beliefs or Expectations**: these often are connected to soul ties, formed through the influence of what you have said, or others have demanded of you. They sometimes come from the tradition of family, or organizations we have participated and /or doctrines of religious sects which are not founded in sound biblical doctrine. Examples: anywhere vows except in marriage as described in the Bible are made, gang membership, any organization which puts anything before God or His Word. An incorrect belief or expectation may insist you vote a certain party from family tradition; you must always honor a pledge made outside of God's expectation, any religion which requires you to be separated from Christian participation, only their church is the right church such as Jehovah's Witness, Mormons, etc. secret groups: Masons, Sororities, etc. Any person, organization, church, religion, denomination, or place which requires you to keep secret, make vows, obey beyond parental knowledge (minor children) or pledge allegiance to anything other than Christ, needs to be repented, and renounced.

4. **Decisions or Vows**: promises to oneself or statements made from false beliefs or wrong expectations. Examples: *"I know I should vote for this person, but my parents have always voted for the other party." "I really don't believe the way those at my church do, I don't think it is in line with the Bible, but I don't want anyone to be upset with me, or break family tradition, so I go along with it."* Or *"I will never speak to them again." "I will never get married."* Any

promise or vow you make that locks you into a place you may not want or should remain.

5. **Word Curses**: Negative things said by you or someone else concerning your character, behavior, physical body, spiritual being, intellect or emotions. Words have power to heal or hurt. The Bible says we will give an account for every careless word we speak on the day of judgement. Our words matter. Think of it this way. If someone says something hurtful, or damaging to one of your children, you wouldn't stand for it! I don't think God will either. Saying things such as, *"I am ugly, I am stupid, I can't do anything right, I will never be out of debt, I will never be happy etc.* Not receiving what God says about you will bring you into a negative view. Reading the first chapter of Ephesians and by making it personal it will give a sense of how God feels about us.

6. **Traumatic Experiences:** these are events where someone suffers tremendous hurt and/or embarrassment, and shame. For example, a young boy has trouble with stuttering and the teacher at school is always putting him in front of the class to speak, of course he is laughed at and made fun of. This causes him shame and he is traumatized and even as a grown man he will suffer from the pain of that rejection. Traumas come in many forms and intensities. Be careful in this arena, if someone has suffered a violent or seriously damaging event, do not try to psychoanalyze them. You are not qualified unless you are a licensed and trained mental health counselor. Take them through forgiveness and spiritual healing according to God's Word. Prayer, and repentance for holding unforgiveness and releasing their pain to Christ can bring divine healing. Forgiving is not saying the offense doesn't matter, it simply says that one chooses to not allow the pain and suffering of that offense to rule their soul.

7. **Evil or Demonic Influence:** this is where it may get a bit uncomfortable but follow the leadership of Holy Spirit. Never call these entities negative names, it will not serve Godly purpose. Remember, you are not just dealing with evil spirits, your agenda is to bring that person to a place of restoration, a place of healing and wholeness. This comes after all the other steps because through repentance, forgiveness, renouncing, releasing and receiving, the demons have nothing in which to stay attached. Through your authority in Christ as a born-again believer and cooperation of the receiver, the demons have no right to stay. There may be some indicators of physical manifestation, however, it is a work of faith, and that faith is grounded in believing God's Word. It does work! Remember, the devil is a liar and a trickster, he will try to convince you he is still operating, choose faith in the finished work of Christ.

Notes

CHAPTER EIGHTEEN

Steps

It is essential to go through each step. Again, ensure you have someone to take notes. They don't have to be extensive; just jot significant things the person receiving ministry may say. This may reveal emotions that need to be dealt with. After the session, the receiver should destroy the notes. Have a small trash container available if the person feels like spitting up. This will not necessarily happen, but don't be concerned if it does. Have on hand tissues, water, paper, and pens.

It is beneficial to ask what medications the person is presently taking. This is to be aware of any situation that may present itself, special needs, or concerns. The person may need to take small breaks more often. Be cautious that it is not abused; the enemy knows his time may be short, and he will use any tactics to divert the ministry. If the person takes any medication that alters their ability to clearly think, such as any anxiety medication, it would be good to do short segments and take a short break, stand, and stretch. The last step needs to be continuous as much as possible without interruption. Remember, we are an entire being constructed of spirit, soul, and body. Each part needs to receive attention and ministry.

Instruct the person receiving ministry if, at any time, they experience pain or discomfort to let you know immediately. They commonly feel pressure in their arms and chest, slight difficulty breathing, or anxiety. If this occurs, stop, calm them down, pray for them, and bind any evil interference. Pray something like, *"Father God, we thank You for this process of freedom. We thank You that* (name the person) *is protected by You. Under Your authority, we bind every evil influence the enemy has on this person. We submit to Your peace in this moment and declare total healing, in Jesus' name. Amen."* This is often a sign of demonic activity. Stay calm. Take a few moments to allow them to pull it together and assure them and yourself that all is well. Remind them of their position in Christ. Never try talking someone into going beyond their ability to endure. You will, however, need to encourage continuance.

This is a voluntary ministry, and we never violate someone's will. Evil will always try to intimidate. As the leader, you must stay alert, watch, and allow Holy Spirit to instruct you. You may witness that sleepiness is not uncommon for any of the team or receiver to experience. If it seems excessive, it probably is a spirit trying to divert the process. Take authority: *"In Jesus Name I bind or forbid any evil spirit from hindering this ministry. Go in Jesus Name."* If necessary, get up and stretch. Remember, body and soul are involved. Minister to both. You may see the receiver throughout the ministry time, especially the last step, yawn, sneeze, cough, or even pass gas. This possibly is a sign of evil spirits leaving. Remember, spirit means air, breath, and wind. Spirits enter through gateways, eyes, ears, mouth, nose, or any bodily opening. Keep your eyes open even during prayer. Open with prayer. Make it your own, but it might go something like the following:

> *"Heavenly Father, we come to you with open hearts that we might receive freedom from anything that keeps us from Your best. Give us wisdom, empower us with Holy Spirit to expose the enemy of our soul. We ask that You station angels about to guard and protect us in the spiritual realm. Give us the ability to move in power without fear or intimidation.*

Saturate us with faith, hope and love. Help us to show strength and mercy to one another as we walk through any darkness to break every assignment of the evil one and embrace Your perfect will for our lives. Amen"

Having the receiver briefly talk about their salvation experience might be beneficial. Many believe they are saved but assume it is because of a family member, or they will say things such as, *"I've always believed in God,"* or *"I been in church all my life,"* or *"I love God."* At any rate, you want to make sure they have a personal relationship with the Lord. Hearing the actual testimony of that event will clear any misconception. If there is doubt, ask them to pray in repentance and accept Jesus for clarity's sake. Throughout the process, the receiver needs to pray aloud.

Have the person write the things they struggle with. I suggest e-mailing a form so the receiver can complete it before the session. They will include things like anger, unforgiveness, jealousy, guilt, shame, condemnation, feelings of unworthiness, fear of failure, hatred, sexual perversions, cursing, or any strong emotion that causes them to falter.

You will find template prayers before each section, but always allow Holy Spirit to guide you. Instruct that although they are repeating after you, they are to trust they are praying from their heart in faith, not just words they are repeating. The facilitator needs to read the words of the prayer in short sentences and have the person pray it aloud. Faith comes by hearing.

Often, you will hear the receiver say something like, *"I don't have enough faith."* Remind them that Jesus is the author and finisher of our faith, and He will see it through. Our reliance is always on Christ, not our ability.

Soul Wounds or Heart Issues:

"Father, I thank You that I can come to You and release all my sin and fears. I repent of _____, I choose to forgive those who have

hurt me because of Your forgiveness. I choose forgiveness for myself for allowing _____ to control me. I renounce all participation with this sin. I release it to You, and I choose not to rehearse the offense. I choose to trust You to bring justice and healing to my soul. I choose to receive Your grace to receive freedom from offense. I receive the power of Holy Spirit to walk in forgiveness, faith, hope, and love. Amen.'

Fill in the blank with the things which have strong influence in your life. Repeat if necessary. You may pray through individual offenses or in small groups of offenses.

Generational curses:

"Father, I choose to forgive all members of my bloodline for anything passed down through to me through their sin or inability to trust You for healing. Any disease that has been inherited through my bloodline ancestors I break its cycle now in the name of Jesus. I choose to walk in freedom from disease as Holy Spirit teaches me to walk in good health as my soul gets healthy. I break any cycle of sinful behavior which comes through my bloodline. I choose to walk in obedience to Christ through submission and repenting of all participation of sin. I take responsibility for any sin I commit and renounce anything received from my past family history through influence of sin or demons. I thank You Lord for setting me and my future generations free from past sins of my ancestors. I choose to walk in obedience to Your commands by the power of Holy Spirit. In Jesus Name. Amen.'

Be specific with names, if necessary. For instance, if diabetes runs on the mother's side, impose mother in the prayer or vice versa. You may hear them say things such as, *"I probably will have heart trouble or diabetes or arthritis because it runs in our family!"* Never take ownership of anything Christ did not give us! Repent of accepting this as something that must be endured.

Ungodly Soul Ties:

"Father, I choose to sever ungodly ties with (name person involved) *_____, for my sin of* (name the offense) *_____. I ask You Lord to move through me for the forgiveness of this offense. I choose through You to forgive them and myself. I relinquish any offense against* (name the person or persons) *_____. I choose not to allow this to have further influence on how I live or what I choose from this day forward. I ask You to work in this person's life and help them be free from any hurt I may have caused them. I receive Your forgiveness and receive the work of Holy Spirit to help me walk in freedom. In Jesus Name. Amen"*

Remember and remind the receiver that while they are breaking ungodly soul ties, the ties that are good and needful between persons such as siblings, spouses, children or other needful relationships are not destroyed. However, getting rid of ungodly soul ties will help to have a healthier relationship. This is especially important if there has been divorce, or out of order relationships.

False Beliefs and/or Expectations:

"Father, I repent for following all information that has kept me from the truth of Your Word. I forgive all people who may have enticed me to follow false beliefs. I renounce anything which may have attached any false beliefs to my soul. I renounce any false expectation that has put me into bondage of any kind. I break all attachments and agreements which deviate from Your truth. I receive Your forgiveness and through that I forgive myself for being deceived. I choose to walk in the freedom You have given me to make Godly decisions. In Jesus name. Amen

If there is a strong sense or memory of a specific area or person attached to that false belief, put that person's name in prayer followed with verbal forgiveness.

Decisions or Vows:

"Father, I repent for making decisions and vows based on false beliefs and wrong expectations. I repent for making vows through defiled information and locking myself into situations which were not Your best for me. I choose to forgive any who have participated and encouraged me to belive false ideas. I take responsibility for my decisions and now choose to break every agreement with those vows and decisions. I renounce every false belief system I participated in. I receive Your forgiveness and choose to allow Holy Spirit to be my guide in making Godly choices. I renounce every vow I have made outside of Your will for my life. In Jesus Name, Amen."

Don't hesitate to name items that created sinful behavior or wrong mindsets, or any vows made outside of God's plan.

Word Curses:

"Father, I repent for believing and speaking every negative and false thing concerning who You have made me to be. I also repent for speaking ill concerning others. I choose to renounce any participation with this behavior. I ask Holy Spirit to teach me how to use words to be a blessing to myself and others. I ask You to heal every broken part of my soul that influences this wrong behavior. I choose through the power of Your forgiveness to forgive myself and forgive any who have participated in this behavior. I renounce all agreements with destructive speech and thoughts. I receive Your forgiveness and healing. In Jesus Name, Amen"

If there are specific people that come to mind with a definite word curse or accusation, pray specifically for that person.

Traumatic Experiences:

"Father, I recognize that nothing is too hard for You. I repent for allowing this event to define me. I choose to allow You to heal every hurt and destructive action taken against me. I repent for allowing this violation to control my life. Because

of Your great love for me, I choose to forgive all those who participated in this violation. I ask You to work on their behalf to bring them to repentance. I release them to You. I ask You to restore my soul and heal my memories so this event will no longer rule my thoughts. Help me to renew my mind with Your love. I break every agreement with hurt and unforgiveness. I receive Your forgiveness and Your healing power. In Jesus Name, Amen."

If there have been significant traumas it would be helpful to name then in forgiving and releasing.

Evil Influences:

"In the name of Jesus, I command every evil entity, influence, or demon to leave me. I break every agreement with evil through unforgiveness, anger and pride. I choose to allow my Father God and Holy Spirit to lead me and guide my life. I no longer give my cooperation to any evil entity or demonic influence to rule my emotions and decisions. Through the authority given to me through Christ Jesus I command every demon to leave me. It is done in Jesus Name. Amen.

It is best to go through each thing listed as evil influences individually: repentance, forgiveness for oneself, renouncing participation, receiving freedom, and releasing Christ.

This is where close attention is on how the receiver responds, anger, bodily actions, yawning, sneezing, coughing, spitting up, feelings of nausea, etc. Don't be alarmed. When a spirit is called out, meaning you may say something like, *"Spirit of depression or heaviness, you must leave in Jesus' Name."* The receiver must also cooperate by repeating this out loud. No one has more authority than the person affected. It may take several times. Spirits do not like to vacate. Stop and ask the receiver what they feel *if nothing seems to be happening.* Often, they will sense something that needs to be said or prayed about. There may need to be further repentance. Don't be intimidated by silence. The spirits must obey your authority in the name of Jesus. At the end of the day, accept your work of Holy Spirit by faith.

Repeat each evil influence the receiver has listed on the form. Keep it simple: don't beg or threaten. Take authority confidently and have the receiver do the same. It works because of Christ.

After this is completed, ask the receiver to describe any feelings, sensations, or thoughts on how they feel. If they express feelings of something gone, a lighter feeling, stop and give thanks to God for freedom. Don't feel intimidated if there are feelings of something not right or nagging feelings of something not right. Explore what that means by asking questions. What is going on physically, or if the receiver strongly hears any thoughts or names. Ask Holy Spirit for insight. Listen to other people on the team for insight. If nothing concrete is noted, pray.

Father God, we thank You for the work of the Spirit in (name the person receiving ministry). *We trust in You and by faith receive all that we have prayed is in effect and will be walked out by faith. If something is lingering of which we need to minister, show us by Your Spirit. In Jesus Name. Amen.*

Stay in a quiet and prayerful mindset for a few moments. If someone has a thought or observation, trust it to be the Lord. Don't be afraid to explore ideas. Sometimes, further repentance or forgiveness is needed. Every spiritual truth is received by faith. People need signs, and sometimes you will get those, but faith rules at the end of the day!

The receiver should be called after the ministry within a day or two. Inquire of any difficulties, concerns, or praise reports. Pray with them and help establish a mentor or person to help disciple them. This is vital to ensure long-term success.

The prayers and instructions given will be used along with the forms the receiver of ministry will fill out and bring to the sessions. You may use the form following and email the form to a person to fill out. As the ministry team prepares for the inner healing/deliverance session, remember to pray for the person receiving the ministry. The enemy of our soul will try to convince us that it is unnecessary. They may even have a difficult time filling out the form. Call them before the session day, pray with them, answer any questions, and encourage them to believe in a great outcome. Make sure they have your number to call if they encounter any difficulties. I promise it will be unusual if they are not tempted to call it off. The enemy does not want us to be free and active in God's Kingdom.

Notes

CHAPTER NINETEEN

Ministry Form/Checklist

Generational Sins and Curses: List any destructive pattern you have seen throughout your family history of which you find yourself dealing with. For example: Mother—jealousy, anger, worry. Father—pride, not providing for family, drug use, alcohol use. Repeating issues such as divorce, child abuse, homosexual tendencies, poverty etc. List health issues which seem run in your family: heart issues, diabetes, cancer, mental illness, depression etc.

_____   _____

_____   _____

_____   _____

_____   _____

Ungodly Soul Ties: List anyone with whom you have unhealthy relationships. List sexual partners (first names only) those of whom you have been married and divorced. Children, especially if there is friction or they are in an unhealthy relationship with you. Any person or groups where your participation has not been healthy or godly, e.g., unlawful acts, gangs, religious groups not living according

MINISTRY FORM/CHECKLIST

to God's Word, cults, Free Masons, secret groups, etc. Breaking ungodly soul ties does not mean the relationship is broken, good soul ties are kept for existing marriage and long-term relationships.

_____   _____
_____   _____
_____   _____
_____   _____
_____   _____
_____   _____

(If extra space is needed, use a notes page)

False Beliefs or Expectations: List any teaching, beliefs against people or groups which are against sound biblical teaching or expectations that has let you down. Examples: Church doctrine or teachings that were not true. Any involvement with the occult or witchcraft. Trusting certain groups and rejecting anything contrary to sound counsel (political, social clubs, religious organization, secret societies, etc. Negative beliefs about yourself. Unrealistic expectations concerning your abilities to succeed.

_____

_____

Decisions or Vows made from false beliefs or expectations: Examples: oaths or vows or allegiances made to any group or systems which kept you from being free to see truth. Statements made which begin with, *"I will never…"*

Word Curses: Negative or hurtful things you or others have said about you concerning your character, behavior, physical body, spiritual being, intellect, or emotions.

Traumatic Experiences: Events or experiences which have caused tremendous hurt or embarrassment or intense shame. These experiences often cause a wall to form between you and your ability to trust God. This could be anything from being embarrassed because of learning disabilities, physical appearance, to severe trauma such as rape, sexual misconduct, poverty, etc.

MINISTRY FORM/CHECKLIST

Evil Influences: Evil influences or demons attach themselves to any emotion or behavior that is not properly dealt with over time. Demons enter through agreements made through our choice of wrong behavior. This does not make one evil; however, it shows great strength in making a choice to get rid of any hinderance which keeps us from walking in freedom. Demons take on the trait of the out of order emotions. What strong emotions or habits keep you locked in a cycle of rebellion, dysfunction, or failure to succeed?

Now that you have willingly participated in your freedom, you must learn to walk it out in everyday life. This was not a magic wand. Through your lifestyle you have trained your soul to make wrong choices. Now because of this prayer and deliverance ministry, you are free to pursue truth and make Godly decisions. You expelled the dark influences, but you will have to retrain your thinking. You need to get into a group of believers, learn what the Word says, keep a heart of repentance toward God, it will take time. Through our Lord Jesus Christ and the continued working of Holy Spirit it will produce victory and fruit for God's Kingdom!

I pray you experience God as never before! Go and bear good fruit for God's Kingdom and enjoy your spiritual journey through experiencing faith, hope, and love!

If you have read this book and not received the gift of salvation or are unsure of your relationship with Christ, this is a simple prayer to use. Understand that it is your faith connected with the finished work of Christ that gives you salvation assurance. Find a church or group of believers that will help you grow and mature in the faith. Pray this out loud and find someone to tell what you have received:

"Dear God, I repent of my sin and believe that You sent Your Son, Jesus Christ, to die for my sins. I believe He was raised from the dead to show me how to have eternal life in Him. Change my heart, teach me how to know You and Your Holy Spirit, which fills me as I receive Your gift of salvation through Christ alone. I praise You for saving me. In Jesus' name, amen."

Notes

How to Read the Bible with Purpose

You may be a beginner at reading your Bible and have little idea of where or how to start. Perhaps you do read but feel frustrated because you feel you are not getting much out of it or how to apply it to everyday life. Your Bible is communication from God to you. It is personal. His heart is not for you to become a Bible expert, but to build relationship with you.

These are simple steps to reading with purpose. If you don't know where to start, read the New Testament first. The Gospels are a good starting place and I suggest Ephesians and Colossians as well.

1. Get a translation that you can understand. The New American Standard and the New English Version are good translation with easy-to-read wording.
2. Set aside at least 15 minutes a day in a place of no interruptions. Try reading a chapter a day. If that is too overwhelming, read half of the chapter. It is not about quantity but quality. It is not a race. Read slowly, read out loud if that helps.
3. Ask yourself these questions:
    a. What jumps out at me? It might be a word, question, or an overall idea. This is Holy Spirit nudging you.

    b. How will this change the way I live my life?
    c. What is my prayer for today? Keep it simple. Prayer is communication, give God a chance to speak to you. Keep a grateful heart and thank Him.
4. Keep a journal, any kind of notebook will do. Write down what you get while reading. Answer the questions above. Write your prayer down and date it. You will be amazed when you see them being answered. You will be able to see your spiritual growth. Be patient with yourself.

"Grace and peace be multiplied to you in the knowledge of God and of Jesus our Lord (II Peter 1:2)."

Author Bio

When you are about to turn 69 years old, it is hard to condense a lifetime of events into a miniature story. Still, I will share with you what you most need to hear that might encourage you to live a life of expectation. Life usually never turns out how we thought it would when we start at twenty!

I will give you the highlights, and they are not all positive! But whose life is? I grew up in a very unstable home with parents who often turned to alcohol for escape. This took its toll on me, my four sisters, and a brother who went to be with the Lord at age 34. It caused all of us to make choices differently.

I married at age 19. I thought it would last forever. It stayed for a long time; looking back, we both had faults that played into that failure. Divorce is painful and ugly, no matter how well you try to do it. I certainly can see where I should have done things better. After 34 years of marriage and at age 52, I found myself on my own. This was a new experience and scary. I made very little money and lived with my wonderful sister and brother-in-law until God provided me a home through another sister. Thank God for sisters! Then God did a crazy thing! He decided I needed to learn to live by faith in my finances.

I have a daughter with two daughters and a son with two sons. Through some difficult circumstances, it became necessary for my

AUTHOR BIO

two granddaughters to live with me. Women have told me how difficult it is to be a single mother, and it is. Still, you should try being a single grandmother and raising grandkids without income! God provided for me in many ways by connecting me with a ministry of which I became part of the ministry team. I will always be grateful for this group of Christ followers. They were not just givers to my finances but also a family to us. At age 60, God decided I was ready for international ministry. To sum it up for space limitations, I just turned 67 in August 2023.

In the short six years from 60-69, I have been to India three times, Honduras once, and Kenya twice, besides traveling to other states in the US to do conferences. I know that I will go to other places in the world before God is finished. God is not really concerned with our age. In February 2018, another game changer came into my life: I met a man. It is a funny story I don't have the space to tell. The following November, we were married!

I chose not to date throughout the 13 years I was single, so getting married was shocking to most people who knew me. I had lived in the Rock Hill and York area of South Carolina all my life. Moving away from there seemed foreign to me. Nevertheless, I moved and currently reside in Cayce, SC, just outside Columbia, with my sweet, husband, Ray Renner. We are probably the most unlikely couple to be together, but God has His own agenda. I have met some wonderful new friends, and God has put me with new ministry partners. Between the two of us, we have 4 children, 9 grandchildren, and 2 great-granddaughters. Life is challenging, and that makes it good!

Be encouraged and enjoy this journey called life! You can't do anything wrong enough to rock God off His throne!

The Fiery Sword Global Ministries

The Fiery Sword Publications

Lexington, SC 29073

www.thefierysword.com

thefierysword@windstream.net

Made in the USA
Middletown, DE
23 September 2023